UNCOMMON APPETITES

Also by Lucy Wilson Sherman

Laying Foundations: A Memoir
A Year Building a Life While Rebuilding a Farmhouse

UNCOMMON APPETITES

Personal Essays

Lucy Wilson Sherman

Madison Press

Susquehanna • Pennsylvania • 2003

Although this is a work of nonfiction, some names have been changed.

ISBN: 0-97428-550-1

Cover photo: Julie Wilson Peierls
Author photo: Henderson Rouse
Book design: Lucy Wilson Sherman

An earlier version of "At a Turn in the Road" was first published in
Creative Nonfiction, Number 8.

An earlier version of "Learning from Goats" was published in *Creative
Nonfiction*, Number 10, and in *On Nature: Great Writers on the Great
Outdoors*, 2002.

An earlier version of "Writing on Mowing" was first published in
Pilgrimage: Reflections on the Human Journey, Volume 23, Number 3,
July-September 1997.

For additional copies:

Heartland Distributors
RR 2, Box 189 B
Susquehanna, PA 18847

For my father, Paul Everett Wilson,
whose generosity made finding a home feasible,
but whose greatest gift was an appetite for life,
uncommon and unbridled.

I want to record how the world comes at me,
because I think it is indicative of the way it comes at everyone.
And to the degree that it is not,
then my peculiarities should strengthen the reader's own sense of
individuality.
Phillip Lopate, *Portrait of My Body*

CONTENTS

INTRODUCTION

" The dread of all publishing companies," writes Phillip Lopate, the high priest of the personal essay, "is to be caught publishing a random collection of pieces." He cannot fathom why the publishing world should be leery of short pieces, short *stories* as well as essays, but he most definitely wants us to know that his thirteen essays, collected in *Portrait of My Body* and published by Anchor books/Doubleday, are related. In the introduction, he writes, "...I am obliged to insist that the book you hold in your hands isn't (shudders!) a random collection...but, for better or worse, a coherent, thematically interconnected work...." In case there might remain some disbelievers, he goes on to tell us what the themes are. They are "carapace of self, detachment, resistance, [and] wariness toward transcendence," esoteric terms that seem varied enough, indeed *vague* enough, to cause a punctilious reader to question the claim of commonality despite his pledge.

But, honestly, who other than the punctilious reader or publisher cares whether or not the essays are thematically related? "If," as Lopate continues, "I am interested enough in the mind of an essayist I will gladly follow him or her anywhere...."

Of course. Who wouldn't? For most readers, the proof is in the print, not the premise.

And on Lopate's last assertion, I could rest the case of my own collection of personal essays. However, on the off chance that one of the people holding this book in her hands is just so punctilious, let me assure her that the themes in the following essays are related. They follow a geographic progression from my childhood home in Maplewood, New Jersey, and a decade in Philadelphia, Pennsylvania, to what I hope is my final home on a farm in Susquehanna, Pennsylvania. They proceed from dark to light and back to dark again, both in substance and in mood. (Note: In order to benefit from their author's cynicism, therefore, you should read them in this order.)

More importantly, they are basted by the conceit of appetite, both metaphorical and literal. The metaphorical is easy—a passion for animals and order and control over events, and a hunger to reside more comfortably within myself. The literal? The first line of the first essay is "When Mother died, I ate her." "Living High on the Bean Sprout," a few essays later, is about rural life as a neo-vegetarian. "Living High on the Hill," its companion piece, is leavened with recipes. In "Writing on Mowing," I bite off more grass than I can chew as I pursue my penchant for order.

But how can a book that begins with "A Lady's Death" and ends in a face-off with death, "The End," be about appetite? Because death is the converse of appetite, the anti-thesis to the thesis of these essays. After all, it is through our appetites that we express our desire to live, and it is through our desires that we manifest our individuality.

Finally, I suspect I have a certain appetite for death itself. What else is a scoured counter, an empty surface, a made bed, a mowed lawn, a finished to-do list—what else is order but cessation? And what is cessation but the absence of appetite? The absence of appetite? Death.

If I could see far enough down the road, if I could write myself around the turn in the road and see into my own demise, perhaps I could enlarge myself enough to incorporate death into my everyday consciousness. Bluntly—*accept* it, damn it! Stop resisting death with the petulance of a child, a stance that merely demonstrates an immature belief in a grand design and, thus, in a grand designer.

It would mean making a home for death inside my life—in a way, swallowing death, making substance out of what is incorporeal. If I could swallow death, could death devour me?

LEAVING HOME

A LADY'S DEATH

When Mother died, I ate her. I drove out to Lord & Taylor in Milburn, New Jersey, where Mother had shopped for years, and sat down for lunch in the Birdcage restaurant, where Mother had measured out her later years as an executive's wife and where the waitresses, who admired her, addressed her formally— Mrs. Wilson—as she preferred. I ordered a chef's salad, without ham, please, and with Italian dressing on the side, if you don't mind. I ordered tea, reminding the waitress politely to be sure the water was "furiously boiling" before pouring it into the teapot. For dessert, I had one of their bird-sized portions of prune whip. After lunch, I browsed in Designer Suits, where I selected a mauve wool suit, a gray silk blouse with a cowl neck to go with it, matching gray sheer stockings, and gray suede pumps.

But it was a strain embodying Mother, and I slumped into a chair with my packages before walking through the exit doors. I returned the suit ensemble and drove home to Riverdale, New York, in time to gather up my daughter, Becky, in my arms as she skipped down the school steps from first grade.

I am qualified to describe my mother's death—how Mother engineered her dying, wanted to die, and was as in control in dying as she had been in life, holding death off until her three daughters, her husband, and her sister could be with her, and then quietly turning inward. But I am less qualified to describe Mother herself, because I've never been able to see who she was apart from my imagined or real unmet needs.

During my childhood, I dreamed of melting into the big blowsy bosom of a black mammy whose imaginary physiognomy was loosely modeled on that of our cleaning women. This dream mammy would fold me into her pillowy breast and rock me, humming Negro spirituals. What I got instead was a thin, high-strung white woman whose love I doubted. When I confessed this doubt to my older twin sisters, my father, friends of the family, they said, why certainly Mother loved me. But, by my hopes, what I received from Mother was not then recognizable as love. In later years, I considered the possibility that my expectations might have been too high, my needs excessive. I hoped that when I fully matured I'd come to see that a constant low *tsk, tsk* of disapproval offset by gifts from Lord & Taylor and Bergdorf Goodman had indeed been love.

I remember as a baby crying in my crib in the white sunroom where I slept. Three walls were windows, and I remember feeling shot through with light, my neediness exposed. No one came to my cries, it seemed, although someone eventually came or I wouldn't have grown up at all. But my wailing went on long enough for me to become convinced of the futility of pleading for solace. Not that I stopped trying after only that one lesson. I hit my head against the wall of my mother until I was seventeen years old and could leave home. I spent the next sixteen years until her death learning that it was equally futile to ask the rest of the world for mothering.

My psychiatrist told me that the term for what I'd become was counter-dependent—so unwilling to appear needy, I faked self-sufficiency. Gradually, I became as domineering as Mother and, when she died, I seemed to swallow up every last bit of her personality. If I couldn't earn or cajole her approval, I could at least create a semblance of security by controlling the events in my life. By becoming just like her, alternately frantic to keep things under control and depleted from the effort, I gained satisfaction from our imagined synchronicity. By becoming her, I kept her alive.

As a teenager, jacked about by hormones, I was often stunningly depressed. I'd beg Mother to listen to my troubles; she'd beg off to make dinner. It seems as if I spent my childhood trying to get her ear.

A suburban housewife in the 1950s, who didn't work outside the home, Mother was intelligent and energetic. It might seem by today's standards that she should have had enough time for clothes shopping, grocery shopping, bridge luncheons, volunteer work, and running the household, with some left over to listen to her youngest daughter. But Mother was thirty-four when I was born and had just gotten her six-year-old twin daughters off to first grade. Maybe she hadn't meant to start all over with another infant.

Mother told me later that when I was a child I had played alone for hours in my room or outside in the backyard. She'd felt a little snubbed by my independence, she said, though I remember those times as being full of longing for her. It was an unfortunate misunderstanding. Still, I imagine she was relieved not to have to put aside her housework for children's games, glad not to relive the powerlessness over people and events that characterizes childhood.

I know *I* certainly hated childhood, although there were some sweet times between us. I remember the distinct Mother-smell of her gray wool sweater with the jewel neckline, along the edge of which lay a strand of perfect pearls. She would take me on her lap and sing to me this song, which I have sung to my own daughter and now my little granddaughter, changing the names: *Who's my Lucy, who's my girl? Little Lucy Wilson is my sweet pearl.*

In those days, children lived close enough to the grade school to walk home for lunch. Mother would fix us a can of Campbell's tomato soup and two liverwurst with red onion sandwiches on Thomas' protein bread. Into her own soup bowl, and even mine, she would occasionally pour a tiny amount of sherry from the decanter. It was a confidential gesture that made me feel adult and special.

The cocktail hour was an important part of every evening when I was growing up. My mother held to four ounces of Canadian Club, but my father relaxed from his day in Manhattan with as much as a third of a bottle of Baccardi rum, mixed with iced water in the summer, hot water in the winter. He never suffered hangovers or missed a day of work. Each morning he rose at 5:30 to take the 7:04 train from Maplewood to Hoboken. There he boarded the PATH tube under the Hudson River to Manhattan, then took a cab to his office on Madison Avenue, where he was vice president and, later, chairman of the board of an international executive search firm.

Sometimes after the cocktail hour, Mother would pass me on her way to the kitchen to make dinner. The times were precious when she paused, put her arms around me, and said, "Don't you know I love you?" It did seem then as if she loved me, but by morning she was back to being exasperated by something, harried and hurried and overwhelmed by all the things on her to-do list.

Like many women of her day, Mother's sphere of power was confined to the house. She had an aptitude with numbers and had once told Daddy she thought she'd enjoy working as a bank teller. With uncharacteristic assertiveness, Daddy put his foot down: "No wife of mine needs to work outside the home." Mother agreed it would be unseemly, but she was smart enough and high-strung enough that without an outlet for her talents, her energies were wasted on repetitive household chores. She scoured counters to within an inch of their life, smoothed the wrinkles from our bedspreads with a slide rule and level. Though I now find myself irritated over other equally minute signs of disorder, I can't produce quite the same lather over woodwork as she did—perhaps because mine is unpainted pine and doesn't show dirt or fingerprints.

The woodwork in the large colonial home I grew up in was white. I knew to keep my grubby hands off it. If my boyfriends didn't, they soon discovered the rules. Awkward and shy, unsure of what to do with their hands while they waited for me in the foyer, they invariably propped themselves up by leaning a hand against the white doorjamb. This was carelessness they wouldn't forget. Mother was there in a flash. She'd suck in her breath, then release it in a pained sigh. Trying to conceal the exasperation in her voice, she'd begin, "I know you don't realize what you're doing, dear, but would you please not put your hands on the woodwork." As if touched by fire, my young friends whipped away their hands, looking down at them accusingly before stuffing them into their pockets where they'd be no more trouble.

"A young man's hands are dirty, dear," explained Mother, "and I have a terrible time keeping the woodwork clean." Walking back toward the kitchen, she'd mutter, "I just don't know why everyone has to put their hands on the woodwork…" Stupefied and shamed, my boyfriends later told me they thought my mother was a little nutty.

Mother had little faith in natural processes. She believed things would get out of hand if she were not vigilant. Each day, she whipped herself into a frenzy trying to accomplish everything on her to-do list. Meal preparations preoccupied her. She planned menus and shopped for the ingredients nearly every day. We had a cleaning woman once a week, but Mother did the laundry and ironed Daddy's business shirts herself. In the days before permanent press sheets, she ironed the bed linens, too, feeding them through a contraption with two large rollers called, improbably, a "mangle." This machine was set up in the laundry room in the basement, where she could sit down at it, but it was time-consuming and futile, like making the beds in the first place. One night of thrashing about on the sheets obliterated her efforts.

In a little account book she kept track of every penny she spent, tallying the columns again and again by hand, fretting if she was off by as little as two cents. She held herself to high moral standards— returning money to the bank the few times a teller made an error in her favor—and high social standards, too—writing her thank-you notes immediately upon receipt of a gift and reluctantly, but dutifully, planning the next cocktail party when she judged that she and Daddy were in debt to friends who'd had them over for drinks.

A routine steadied her; change upset her excessively. Her travel through life was not easy—she stayed only sixty-six years.

I was thirty-three when she died. I may have scoffed at her idiosyncrasies when I was younger, but she's had the last word. A mother wins. You can grow up to become her opposite, but that no more reflects your independence from her than growing up, as I have done, in her image.

Mother lived by lists. In later years, my sister had large, white pads made for Mother, each page beginning with two lines of print in the top left-hand corner: Make Beds. Do Dishes. I know for a fact there were times when Mother would add to the list already completed items in order to savor the tiny burst of satisfaction produced by crossing them off.

I understand the lists. Once her life was down on paper—the errands, the laundry, the returning of dresses to Lord & Taylor or B. Altman—the list took on a life of its own. Once it was written down, no one could accuse her of not doing anything all day. There it was as proof that she counted, and she passed or failed the day depending on how many items on her list she crossed off. (I have joked that on my tombstone will be engraved *my* last list. A short one. Only the word D I E , followed by a triumphant check.)

On the infrequent occasions when she was too tired to make dinner, we played hooky from our real lives and Daddy took all five of us to the Chinese restaurant. Or, sometimes, when Daddy was out of town on business and the twins were in college, Mother and I sneaked over to Howard Johnson's for tuna melts and hot fudge sundaes. Daddy would never have begrudged us the expense of a meal out and, as Mother controlled the purse, might never have known. But Mother considered it an extravagance. By the next evening when I came home from school, she'd be recovered from the lapse and standing over the stove, arching her head back to prevent the steam from the cooking vegetables from frizzing up her perm.

Mother never wore a pair of pants in her entire life. Before we hired the cleaning women, she did the housework in pale plaid cotton dresses and comfortable lace-up oxford shoes called "clodhoppers." She kept a pair of navy pumps in the kitchen to change into if anyone called at the front door. She wore a girdle and stockings all year long except on the very hottest summer nights, when she wore only a petticoat over her garter belt and stockings.

She believed in behaving as she ought to, resisting her natural longings. I came to see that it was her effort to keep from knowing she even had longings that made her suppress my spontaneity, ignore my adolescent fears, and disapprove of my budding sexuality. Mother's unconscious had to be as organized as her attic—nothing messy or ill fitting could be tolerated—and my teenage need for endless listening must have seemed extremely messy and certainly ill fitted to her daily schedule.

It took me years to accept that there was no getting from Mother the particular quality and quantity of attention I needed. Before she died, I had become enough like her to finally win at least her acceptance. She loved me all she was ever going to and, in the end, it was enough.

I would drive out from Riverdale to Maplewood every other week to lunch with her at Lord & Taylor's while my daughter was in school. During my visits, her habits and compulsions held sway. Things that occupied her thoughts were a broken fingernail, the laundry that needed folding, unanswered correspondence, an incident at the Planned Parenthood clinic in Newark, where she had volunteered as a receptionist once a month for seventeen years. I followed her around while she chatted. She had never wanted to hear much about my marriage and so was taken by surprise when I told her my husband and I were separating.

We discussed easy, light topics. Although it was just Daddy and her at home now, meal preparations still consumed her; by the time the breakfast dishes had been done (which involved not only washing but drying every one of them, putting them away, and then scouring and drying the black marble counters), it would be time to worry about lunch and then dinner. A grocery store run necessitated bathing, pulling on a different girdle, a clean pair of stockings, and a navy sheath, and applying a line of red lipstick and a spritz of Youth Dew by Estee Lauder.

I am my mother during the daylight hours. At night, with all my chores and duties discharged, I am my father. It is my father who dissolved in laughter and in tears and who seeded my appetite for good food and enthusiastic sex. I must have gleaned from him a naturalness about my body and, when I hit puberty, I thrust straight toward sex. It was puberty that fatally divided Mother and me. Mother was not in favor of sex. I, most ardently, was. There was no cerebration to my actions then; only in retrospect do I see that sex made an excellent corrective to the dreariness of days measured by accomplishment.

Although Daddy bequeathed me the great gifts of laughter and lust, Mother gave me everything else. Bit by bit, it dawns on me how vast is the gift of "everything else."

I hardly needed my grammar classes, Mother's speech was so correct. She prided herself on using words precisely. She never misused the words *lie* and *lay*, and both she and Daddy winced and rolled their eyes each time they heard the commercial, on our tiny, new black and white TV, that proclaimed, "Winstons taste good *like* a cigarette should."

My taste in clothing and home decorating is impeccable—it's hers. I am pro-choice and disapprove of large families. I also disapprove of obesity, although this judgment puts me in something of a quandary as my own body relaxes into middle age. I am never late for appointments, return borrowed books on time, and always write my thank-you notes. I buy dark-leafed lettuce, never iceberg. I like the water for my tea furiously boiling. And I firmly believe if I just get up early enough and work hard and fast enough, I can get it all done.

Being so like Mother, I imagine that she spent each day proving to herself that she was not bad. That's the way it is for me. I start each morning from a minus position and try to work my way up to zero by the end of the day. Then I start all over again the next day. Perhaps, if I'd been nurtured more and disapproved of less, life would not be such a Sisyphean ordeal. But Mother didn't have much to spare, the way I see it. She made her life so bone-narrow that, in the end, dying was the only way to escape the rules she wrote around herself.

Although she was a reduced person by the time she died— reduced to one room in a hospital, reduced to weighing less than I, reduced to being interested only in managing the walk from her bed to the bathroom and to having her fingernails filed just so—she died like a lady and with the same control with which she'd lived.

I'd seen dead people before, during an eleven-month stint in nursing school, and I'd seen people so sick they soon would be dead, but Mother permitted us—her daughters, her husband, and her sister—to see the actual steps of dying. She taught us how you go from life to death. You take three long breaths, spaced so far apart you'd think someone couldn't survive in the airless gap between them. It's simple, if you have cancer and pneumonia and feel the house is getting too much to handle.

The attic was her biggest problem. She kept things: meticulously labeled boxes of linens; fine fabrics in mothballs; Christmas decorations; shoes for summer and shoes for winter; letters from her girls away at camp; empty boxes from Lord & Taylor, Bergdorf Goodman, Saks Fifth Avenue, and B. Altman, labeled Empty Boxes; ribbons and used wrapping paper, ironed and folded to be used again; and small leather-bound notebooks of lists, lists of what she'd given us each Christmas since 1942, lists of everyone she'd ever sent a Christmas card to.

She always wanted one of us girls to help her clean out the attic. We'd arrange to have our children met after school, then drive out to New Jersey and spend the day with her up in the attic. In the end, though, she would convince us everything was too important to discard. I suppose if she'd ever cleaned out the attic, given all the stuff to Goodwill, there would be one less large item on her endless list. With less to do each day, her sense of purpose might be jeopardized. Anyway, she never did. She died instead, and Daddy cleaned it out easily later because, after all, the boxes were all labeled.

Mother wasn't afraid of dying, and she wanted either to be well enough to tackle the attic or to die and be done with it. She told her doctor she was thinking of committing suicide. She was in the hospital then, and she talked very reasonably about it. To his credit, he took her seriously, quietly allowing her to examine aloud the various methods. Finally, she decided it would not be fair to Daddy or her daughters to use their cars for dying. To go down the elevator, into the hospital parking lot, turn on the engine, and wait. Or maybe she meant to wait until she got out of the hospital to do it in the garage at home. She wasn't losing her mind and certainly would have realized it would go more quickly in an enclosed space. Anyway, she felt it would be horrible for any one of us to find her dead in our car. Her doctor agreed, and they let it go at that.

She scoffed at people who called death "passing away." She didn't go for euphemisms, except about living bodily functions. For sweating, she substituted "perspiring," even "glowing." For farting, she said "making smells." Both subjects caused her deep embarrassment, especially the latter, but death she greeted bravely. We used the obituary she herself had written. It was a small, factual announcement, omitting the popular term "beloved," which she felt might be presumptuous.

Her dying started with an excruciating pain in her right cheek. Not Tic Douloureaux, the doctors said. She had CT scans and angiograms, in and out of the hospital. They never found out what had caused the pain, although she was laced with cancer when she died and her lungs were filled with fluid. Pneumonia was the actual cause of death and the reason why her last breaths took so long.

We were taking shifts at Columbia-Presbyterian Hospital in Manhattan. Her sister, Betty, stayed with her all day at the end. Betty, whose children were grown and whose husband had died, spent all day watching her sister die. She was terribly sunny about it. She brought her knitting and watched the soaps and shouted at Mother as if she were retarded. (By that time, Daddy and Betty were living together in the big house. Mother had given Betty her own key. Betty and Daddy went on living together after Mother died. Within weeks, Betty had moved into Mother's bed. A year later, they married and sold the house.)

Daddy drove Betty to the hospital on his way to the office and left work early to spend several hours with Mother every afternoon. All the time he was with her, Daddy rubbed Mother, rubbed her feet and hands and back. She never had a bedsore because we all rubbed her smooth, soft buttocks. We helped her prepare the chalky dietary supplement ordered by her doctor because the smell of real food made her nauseated. Mother knew the proper usage of the words *nauseated* and *nauseous*, *nauseous* being something someone else may find you to be. (She was not without occasional self-deprecating humor.) That Mother, who quipped that she had lived to eat, found the smell of food offensive was one of the major signs she was seriously ill.

She was not modest in front of us girls and once, when my daughter and I were visiting her in the hospital, she took off her robe and nightgown near the chair by the window and slowly walked, naked, across the room to the bathroom. Becky and I had time to stare at her body while she concentrated on negotiating the painful steps. Her thinness took our breath away. We'd never seen anyone so thin, except in news clippings of starving people in Third World nations. This was our mother and grandmother, once full and tall. Total strangers used to approach her on the street in our village and compliment her on the fineness of her skin. She was a regal woman, accustomed to fitting her elbow into a silk padded elbow support so the saleswoman at B. Altman's glove counter could work kid gloves down over her long, slender fingers.

I was glad Becky could see Mother like this—less intimidating than when she was well—and that we could get a glimpse into dying. We were not a sentimental family, and it is likely that if Mother hadn't determined to die at the relatively young age of sixty-six, we would have trundled her off to a nursing home when she became awkward to care for at home, and some nurse would have had the education of seeing her naked and watching her take her last three breaths.

On the day she died, all five of us were in the room. It was the first and only time we were all there together. That's how well Mother arranged it. She managed to hang on until my sister Julie trained in from Long Island, although it wasn't Julie's scheduled day to visit and the doctor had said Mother could last for months. But the private duty nurse Daddy hired around the clock said Mother would go soon. She said it with such authority that we believed her. Daddy and Betty were there. Our other sister, Penny, had come over from New Jersey, and I had driven down from Riverdale, leaving Becky in the care of our friend Tina, who had been Becky's camp counselor for two summers and, mature for her years, had become my friend, too.

Mother was in a chair by the side of the bed when I arrived. Julie was helping her take small sips of water. There were no needles in her, and she was wearing her own nightgown, pink, I think. But her eyes were funny. Her lids were half down, drooping. She seemed preoccupied with something internal that we couldn't reach. We got her back into bed, and I remember there was some jockeying to be the one to actually help her lie down.

It was noon. Daddy had brought sandwiches and Dubonnet for lunch. We stood around Mother's bed table, which we had swung into the center of the floor, and unwrapped the sandwiches and poured the Dubonnet over hospital ice in paper cups.

Then Penny turned back toward Mother and said quietly, almost wistfully, "I think Mommy's taking her last breaths." As if rehearsed, each of us moved swiftly to her bedside, her three daughters lining up on one side, Daddy and Betty on the other.

There were two more breaths. In the pauses, the long, long pauses, we wept, all talking at once to Mother through our tears, and we rubbed her. We chanted, "We love you, Mommy, we love you," again and again. There was a long slow heaving of her chest, her eyes sunk back. We rubbed her arms and legs and feet. We wished her well. We told her how much we loved her again and again. We held each other and stroked her body until we knew, by looking into each other's faces, that this pause was the last.

Gradually, we moved back to eating and drinking the Dubonnet, still weeping. We each made our farewells to Mother before we left her bedside and then returned again and again, sandwiches or cup in hand, to stroke her. I wanted to feel how long it took for her to grow cool. I kissed her soft, soft cheek and said goodbye.

We'd never done this before, and we didn't know how to behave. By dying, by relinquishing her grip on life and her requirements of us, Mother gave us permission to do it our way. It was a wake. It was a play, and Mother was the star. With such great emotion there was license, impunity. There were no rules. There was nothing that could touch or hurt us so.

We went on talking about her and eating around her for minutes and minutes before Daddy realized that the hospital staff should be told. He went out and brought back a nurse, who reached over and tried to close Mother's one half-open eye. I remember feeling something primitive and furious rise up in me, a burning in my throat and cheeks, and was glad when the eye wouldn't close. For whom was she closing this eye, when everyone Mother loved had just watched her die? When the nurse asked us to leave, I snarled a "No" that caused her to leave instead. Finally, Mother's doctor came in. After commiserating with us and congratulating us on our unusual openness in the face of death, he explained that they were now going to undress Mother, wrap her in a sheet, and put her in a bag, and that we might as well wait across the hall. We did. We neglected to take her wedding rings from her finger.

Mother's death was a relief. Something final and momentous had happened, and now we could get on with life. We left the hospital together but got into separate cars and drove to separate homes. We never thought to remain together for support that first night. I drove home to Becky and Tina. Tina and I drank wine, and they both put their arms around me. We all cried together.

Finally, we put Becky to bed, and Tina and I stayed up late, drinking wine and talking on about Mother. Tina hugged me and stroked my long, long hair and stood by my chair, her breast by my cheek, and I turned my face and kissed her breast through her blouse. And when she put her hand on my breast and helped me out of the chair and onto the bed, where she made me come in great sobbing, wrenching spasms, I dimly heard a shocked and reproving voice, but the solace of new mothering was louder and more true.

AT A TURN IN THE ROAD

There we were, taking the long way home through the park, Toby, my black lab, bounding on ahead, doing two miles for every one of ours. Lovers we were, holding hands when we weren't struggling single file over rocks and roots. Lovers, inhaling the autumn afternoon, conscious only of the tromp and slide and crunch of our footsteps—and the silence. Lovers. Hardly killers.

The path narrowed so that one of us would hold the branch for the other, then gradually the old logging road, now weedy and rocky from disuse, widened to the width of a car. And there, quietly edging upon our consciousness, was a car facing us in the turn of the road, with its motor running.

At a moment like this you become embarrassed, feeling as if you've been discovered at something. Discovered just being unself-conscious, maybe. You pull yourself out of your reverie, out of your private joke.

You think, Damn, people, intruding upon our afternoon, our privacy. Then you're embarrassed for whomever you're going to come upon. You think, lovers, maybe, necking, or more. You think, oh, someone's just gone to take a leak. You think, maybe there's a dead body in the front seat.

You prepare your face.

Your lover takes the left side of the car and you take the right, the branches and tall weeds forcing you to pass close to the car. It's an old, gray, nondescript car, four doors, some rust along the fender you can see out of the corner of your eye. Of course you try not to look, but the car is running and you glance in as you brush past sideways.

There's a body, a guy on the front seat, curled up fetal fashion, asleep. So, he's got a right. But the car is running. You think, he's gonna suffocate, no windows open, car running—he'll be dead before he wakes. You look over the roof of the car at Rob, who hasn't given in to curiosity, who hasn't looked.

And now you're behind the car and you glance back and see the hose attached to the tail pipe, and, by God, just like in some movie, just the way it would be in that movie we've all seen in our heads, the hose goes around on Rob's side and you say, "Rob," who has passed by now, and your heart is pumping with excitement (this is real life) and fear, and you follow the hose around to the other side of the car and sure enough the hose goes into the front door and you realize what's happening and again, urgently, you say, "Rob," and finally he turns and sees.

So you realize there's a guy in there who has hooked up a hose to the tail pipe of his car and the hose enters the front door and...he's doing it. He's actually doing it, just as you imagined when you hear how people kill themselves in their garage by turning on their car and waiting. You've pictured yourself doing it. Well, by God, there's a guy doing it right out here in our park, broad daylight—well, afternoon, a glorious afternoon, your much-needed afternoon with Rob, unself-consciously melding with nature—and suddenly you're sharp and distinct from the bushes and trees and you think you should do something. Deal with this. You want to enter the drama but simultaneously resent that it has upstaged your own private, low-keyed, small, lover drama.

I have to enter the drama. I have to open the door. There's a temptation, a pull, a seductiveness to being in the presence of someone who's actually doing it. I want to see what it's like, although I'm scared now. Someone who's actually doing it is scary. Maybe it's done already, but then just seeing death is scary.

My hand is on the door and now I've opened the door, stepping back quickly into the bushes. Fear makes me sound angry.

"Hey, what are you doing? What's going on here?" I sound like a cop.

Slowly, groggily, the guy lifts his head. He's alive, although his pale eyes looking up into my face are clouded, unfocused. He's youngish, with stringy reddish-blond hair, a blond mustache. He looks like someone I would know.

"Leave me alone," he mumbles.

"Well…uh…I can't, you see," I answer nervously, with a little laugh, just as if we're having this perfectly natural conversation. Toby's worrying a stick to death over near Rob.

"Go on away. Leave me alone." He's struggling to prop himself up on the steering wheel. It's a struggle, not only because he was on his way out but because his gut is wedged in by the wheel.

"What are you doing, buddy?" Now I sound overly jovial. Rob has finally come back, but because he's still standing a little way off, as if about to run, I feel he must know something. His glasses are winking in the sun; I cannot see his eyes. Maybe somehow I've spoiled our afternoon by having to look. Maybe Rob is angry. Now I'm torn. This guy doesn't want me, and Rob wants to go home. He keeps shuffling, hands stuffed into the pockets of his jeans, shoulders hunched. He keeps glancing toward the paved road. It's silent here in the park except for this shuffling, the thrum of the car motor and Toby still humbling that stick. There's no one else around and we can't see the main road from here. I think maybe I've created this.

"What are you doing?" I can't seem to think of anything else to say. He's looking straight ahead, up the path deeper into the woods, one arm hanging onto the steering wheel for support, thick, nicotine-yellowed fingers (he's a lefty) tapping on the dash, no wedding ring. Then I see the case of Budweiser on the floor in the back, crumpled Camels and some dirty laundry on the seat.

"Why so much beer?" There are empties tossed onto the floor in the front, and his cigarette is still lit in the ashtray. There's something forlorn about that cigarette burning, waiting to be dragged on, life going on.

"It's for the people who find me." His words are slurred. "So they can have a real party when they find me. Now shut the door an' leave me alone."

That part about the people who'll find him drinking his case of beer ticks me off. I shift my weight and look at Rob.

"Rob, what'll I do?"

"Get his keys."

"Aw, shit, just shut the fucking door. Get the fuck away from me."

More minutes of silence while I look back and forth between the guy and Rob. The guy stares out the front window, fully upright now. Rob is impatient. He shuffles a little farther from the car, a little closer to the main road. I think, this guy means business. I picture wailing sirens, cop cars, flashing lights, the ambulance, all that noise breaking into this guy's final moments. This thing he's doing is as private as masturbation. This guy is serious, and I am timid before him. I have never done anything so deadly serious. Now I am moved. I do not want the cops with their sirens and stretchers and their loud bullying voices to disrespect this man and rush him unwilling to a hospital and pump out his stomach, or whatever they do for carbon monoxide poisoning, and treat him as if he doesn't mean it. I am sobered. This is no joke. I think he means it.

And I have no words of hope for him. I have my own problems and my own doubts. What he's doing makes me want to glance behind me, over my shoulder, as if he knows something about life I don't. As if he's leaving a bad party and by leaving makes me see how dreary it really is. What's so great about taking a walk in the park with your supposed lover? I mean, it doesn't solve anything. Nothing at all. It's irrelevant, really, when you consider all the times in life when things go wrong. This party stinks.

I know what I would do if Rob were not here. I would gently close the door on the hose, being careful not to shut off its supply of noxious gas. I would raise my hands, palms forward, to show I meant no harm, and, crouching, I would back away.

"Keys. Get his keys," says Rob, suddenly efficient, crisp, though still standing down toward the main road, out of the guy's sight.

His words galvanize me and now it becomes a game. Will I dare to reach in past the guy (maybe death will grab me too) and pull his keys out of the ignition? That will spoil it for him, inconvenience him, when, after all, if he's gone to this length, he's probably been troubled enough in life.

"We'll put the keys at the end of the road. That'll give him time to think it over." Rob has it figured out now.

"But I don't want to inconvenience him." Rob and I are talking the way you do in front of a child. We're talking as if he's already dead.

"Tell her to shut the door, Rob." He's heard me call Rob's name. "What the fuck do you think you're doing? Both of you, leave me alone." His voice is weary. I understand.

"I'm sorry, but I have to do this."

"Get the fuck away. I've got something in the back seat that'll make you get away." He straightens up, his left hand on the steering wheel, his right arm over the back of the seat.

Oh shit, what's he mean, "something"? A gun, under all those clothes? This man, so free with his own life, would not have the usual compunction.

Quickly, I reach in and pull the keys straight out of the ignition, thinking if they stick, he'll grab my arm and pull me in to where he's going. But they don't stick and I get them and start backing away, apologizing.

"Aw, shit, what are you gonna do with my keys?"

High on my courage, I run to catch up with Rob, whose long legs are carrying him toward the road at a great rate. He calls back, "We'll leave them at the end of this road. You'll have to come and get them, see?" And to me he says, "This will give him time to get some air and think it over."

"How will I find them?" the guy yells. I turn to Rob, who seems to have done this many times before, so sensible is his idea, whereas I just wanted us to figure out a way not to inconvenience the guy, to leave him with his dignity.

"We'll leave them on" (we're striding away now and calling back, and then Rob sees a beer can) "on a beer can" (fitting).

"What?"

We do it. Set the empty can on end in the tall weeds and carefully place the keys so he can see the can and the keys when he gets here.

I shout, wanting to be helpful, "They're on a beer can."

And then we start up the main road. Toby abandons his stick when we call. We leash him now and quicken our steps. After all, anything can happen—he could be hit by a car—we want him close to us. Death is breathing down our necks.

As we reach the top of the hill, we hear, "Rob, where're the keys?"

I turn, see him, and make exaggerated motions toward the can, wanting to be helpful. It's all I can do now. I want him to know we care. We want him to have a good experience. At least that's the way it is for me. Rob and I are not talking now, just high-tailing it home.

We think he finds the keys. There is silence again; it has closed over behind us.

To Rob I say, breathless, "I don't want to call the police. I believe a person should be allowed to make this decision."

I believe in suicide. I believe in death with dignity, and I believe each person ultimately knows his own course—at least we must operate on that premise. When I'm old or sick, I want a pill. And when I die, I'd like my family around me. I'll take the pill with all of them there, so they can watch, so they won't be so afraid for themselves. We were at my mother's bedside when she took her last three breaths. We watched and wept, but it was good to see. Her dying then became a part of my life, and now I am not so afraid. Only, *I* want to say when.

I am exhilarated. The adrenaline is pumping through my very alive body. We march home quickly as evening comes on.

"I don't want to call the cops, Rob."

He does not protest, and I, proud I have stuck by my principles, which were only words before, do not open myself to their challenge and possible overthrow.

I am saddened by what has happened. I did not know I would decide like this. I thought surely my heart would bleed. The rush I used to get from rescuing people has diminished over the years, as I begin to save myself.

I am too charged to eat dinner. We talk about it; we tell my daughter, Becky. Neither Rob nor Becky says, "Let's call the police." Perhaps I present the story in such a way that they see it my way. They agree that, by God, he got as far off the road as he could—he really didn't want us to find him and stop him. We shouldn't have happened along. "The guy intruded on our afternoon," says Rob, almost shouting. I think he's nervous, but I really don't know. He does not discuss his feelings.

We wonder if we could be said to be accomplices. We talk in hushed voices without turning on the light over the dining room table. Maybe, with the breath of fresh air, he won't do it. After all, whom do we know who really means business, who sticks by what he believes? Life is so lukewarm; you are so little called upon to put your money where your mouth is. You can get by in a half-life without ever taking a stand or even being fully awake. You can hedge and compromise. There's so much wasted time in life, so many unaccounted-for hours, so much dross. And here's this guy doing it. He has stature, in my eyes, integrity, calling it quits when it's no good any more rather than selling out, biding his time until death taps him.

I do not ask myself, is his despair only momentary? Is it merely a transient state that I should wheedle him out of? Or an inverted act of aggression which I have a responsibility to stop? I do not ask myself these things, and it is only many years later that it occurs to me that the beliefs I'm so proud of may have blinded me to the particularities of the man before me. In taking for granted that this man's action was deliberate and considered and grew out of his principles, I was making the solipsistic assumption that he was no different from me.

I prepare for bed, a clear purposefulness to my actions. Each motion is precise, distinct from every other motion. I pay attention to what I'm doing and wonder if it's worth it—that is, what it is he knows that I only suspect. His choosing death has brought me closer to the narrow edge of my own life, and I wonder if he doesn't have a point.

The next morning, without a word between us, we know we want to go back and see. I'm rooting for him to have done it, but I don't tell Rob that.

We retrace our path down the hill by car and when we reach the dirt road, we see the car. Holy shit. This has the throb of reality. I'm always wondering when reality is going to kick in.

There are no sounds except Nature going on about her mindless business and the crunch of our footsteps on dry leaves as we creep up to just behind the car and there, with one quick look, we see him lying fetal fashion on the front seat. The hose is connected to the tailpipe and leads into the front door. The engine has run down.

We retreat fast and drive home. Now, now, Rob calls the police.

We make breakfast and wait. Then we hear sirens in the distance. He can't hear them now. It is over. I am shivering with exhilaration and awe and horror at myself. I feel proud of him, although I am aware that others might not applaud what he has done, what we have not done.

Lovers we were, not killers. But not saviors either.

MAKING A HOME

LIVING HIGH ON THE BEAN SPROUT

I f you're in your fifties, like me, and are a former beatnik/hippie type, you might have been seduced by the back-to-the-land movement of the 1960s. You might have dreamed that moving to the country would simplify and order your days and lead pretty directly to spiritual enlightenment. You'd read *Walden* or, if not, you would when you got there. You'd heard about Helen and Scott Nearing and how they built dozens of stone houses, just the two of them, first in Vermont and then in Maine. How they ate raw vegetables, peels still on, plunked down in the middle of their wooden slab table. Cold meals, hard physical labor in the mornings, reading and writing in the afternoons. You knew if only you could quit your job and move to the country, you, too, could live the good life.

That was the dream my husband, Henderson, and I followed, although it took us until the mid-1980s to arrange it. We shopped for property and found 71 acres of sloping hillside along a dirt road with southwestern exposure—20 acres of meadows, 51 acres of woods—

in northeast Pennsylvania. There was an old abandoned farmhouse on the land with three tall pines in front. We were still youngish (42), and by owning and restoring property in Philadelphia, we'd become weekend carpenters. We quit our jobs and moved in just as winter struck, camping out in the kitchen while we demolished and rebuilt the other five rooms around us.

The complete renovation of this nineteenth-century farmhouse, inside and out, took six years, during which time we also learned to cut our own wood, cook a Thanksgiving turkey in the bottom of our wood-burning stove, and make do without running water for the first seven months.

Every myth that had propelled us to the country in the first place exploded before the year was out. We tried, and failed at, every attempt at self-sufficiency and, although I wouldn't have missed a moment of it for the world, we didn't get enlightened—we went broke.

We thought, as many people new to the country do, that we could rent our hayfields to local farmers to cover our real estate taxes. That first summer, as I forced my way down through the meadow on daily walks, the grasses locked tendrils around my waist. Our smaller dog disappeared entirely, leaving dark swaths of folded grass in her wake. I called five local farmers before finding one who might be able to get over to hay our field after he did his own holdings. He'd gotten along without our hay all these years; there was never any question of *his* paying *us*.

Still, I was so grateful at the prospect of striding easily across our land again that when Clarence and his tractor pulled into our yard, I lay down flat on my back in the driveway. He could take me right then and there and, afterward, the hay. After three exhausting, heatstroke-inducing mid-August days, he left, taking only the hay.

In payment, I filled up the front seat of his pickup with a variety of the healthy foods we neo-vegetarians had on hand: dense, whole-wheat pastas; soy and rice milk dairy alternatives; salt-free, oil-free tortilla chips; *fun*-free cookies; peculiar condiments with foreign names and obscure applications; and more beans and grains than he'd ever use, considering he was a dairy farmer who drank raw milk and butchered his own pigs and steers each year. All this totaled about $75, so we ended up paying our real estate taxes plus $75 to get our fields hayed, and considered ourselves lucky.

Our first purchase after the closing on the property was a wood-burning stove. Our second was a lightweight and reliable chainsaw. We followed every single piece of advice in the manual and gradually learned to fell trees, starting out with small trees—saplings, really and eventually conquering our fear enough to tackle some serious ones. Without machinery to get the logs out of the woods, we tied one end of a rope to the tree trunk and the other end around our waists, and hauled, like horses, one log after another down the mountain and into the clearing where we could cut them up and throw them into the trunk of the car. Although it's not something we thought about when purchasing the farm, the woods are, thankfully, uphill from the house, so the slope to the woodpile is conveniently *down.*

With so much money going to house renovation and zero coming in, we began to eye our woods differently. We'd sell off standing timber to lumberyards. They would take the long straight trees and leave us the tops for firewood. We spent the better part of a day walking our 51-acre woodlot, first with a forester and then with several representatives from lumberyards and pulp mills. Our trees, all second growth, were not big enough to be turned into boards, so the lumber yard wasn't interested, and 50 acres does not offer a paper mill enough pulp, short of clear-cutting the entire mountain. We believe that by the time we're 80 our stand may be ready to throw off several thousand dollars to my daughter, who, by then 60, will probably have made her own way.

One early spring day a neighbor came by, looked up at our ancient orchard of eight hollow apple trees, and told us our soil lacked boron. He gave us this tip: Buy 20 Mule-Team Borax and sprinkle one box around the perimeter of each tree.

Skeptical, I nevertheless went to the Acme the next day and bought eight large boxes of the stuff and did as he'd instructed. Lo and behold, that fall, brilliant red and yellow King apples crowned the branches of these almost entirely hollow trees. Naturally we attributed the bounty to our neighbor's advice, but later learned that apples are plentiful every seven years or so, with or without Borax, and 1986 was a particularly favorable year for apples all along the eastern seaboard.

I asked my family for a cider press; we thought we'd try the apple cider business as a small source of income. The press came unassembled, as did everything else in this do-it-yourself period. (Assembling things that come in boxes with directions, translated from the Japanese by people fluent only in Urdu and diagrammed by sleep-deprived sadists, causes divorce among couples who depend less upon each other for survival than we did.)

Henderson climbed into the branches and beat the apples down with a stick while I ran around below collecting them, bobbing and ducking to avoid being bopped, and thinking of Newton. We sat on the porch and cored the apples, ignoring the blisters that quickly appeared on our index fingers. We took turns turning the crank that ground the apples before scooping the pulp into a mesh bag and twisting down on the press. I could twist down only so far before running out of strength. It took Henderson's muscles before the mash produced a drop of liquid. By the end of one entire day of this, we had a mountain of pulp and eight gallons of cider—one measly gallon per tree. It was not a process we ever wanted to repeat. The $275 cider press serves nicely as a planter in one corner of the living room.

The following year, we filled up the trunk of the car with cartons of apples and drove to a nearby cider mill—a large, metal shed where the engine of a tractor drove the press. We backed in the car, dumped our apples into an enormous vat, cores, stems, bruises, worms, and all and, for a half-hour, took turns holding more than two dozen gallon jugs under a thin but steady stream of sweet nectar—cider from our own trees for only $.35/gallon.

The simple life is one of extremes. The harvest inundates you as surely as the winter months deplete you. Two dozen gallons of cider were more than we could possibly consume (if you don't drink cider within a week, it turns "hard," and after that, it becomes vinegar) so, on our way home, we dropped off a gallon each to eight neighbors, a gallon each to the salespeople at the hardware store, the lumberyard, and our auto mechanic, all of whom had been helpful in getting us through that first year.

That night, we taught ourselves to pasteurize the rest of the cider by canning it. (Canning means putting something into a glass jar with a tight lid. Go figure.) The purpose of pasteurizing is to kill the microorganisms that cause fermentation. The result is not cider but apple juice, which has a long shelf life.

Because we had no conventional stove (we cooked with only a microwave oven and a wood-burning stove for the first four years), we devised a complicated but effective procedure to raise the temperature of the cider by heating it in a water bath on the wood-burning stove and adding water boiled in the microwave to keep it steady for the prescribed length of time. The result was 20 quarts of apple juice. Apparently it was botulism-free, because we drank it all and are still here to tell the tale.

Now that we'd mastered apple growing, apple picking, and apple cidering, a world of other labor-intensive projects opened before us.

How about a Christmas tree business? That first spring we took several days from our renovation schedule to plant, with two friends, 800 free pines and spruces in the lower field between our house and our neighbors'. Even if we didn't get rich selling them, in time the trees would obscure the sulfur floodlight the neighbors had erected against the total blackness of a country night.

So, during an inevitable spring drizzle, we planted. Free seedlings are one size up from embryos; 800 of them can easily be packed into two large cardboard boxes because what you're planting are, essentially, hairs.

Grab a hunk of your own hair. Each strand is a little tree. Separate out one strand, pluck it, go out back, take up a pick, heave it up over your head and plunge it into the earth. Now make the hair stand up in the hole, stuffing the dirt in around it, but making sure its little bottom doesn't bend. Do this in a drizzle. Do it 200 times (my share of 800 trees divided by four people). Plant about a third of the hairs in what will turn into a small stream, in a few weeks, drowning all the seedlings in its path. After the spring rains, there will be the major drought of 1988, which will kill three-quarters of the rest. By the year 1995, what you have left are about 100 waist-high white pines, which, nobody told you, don't make very nice Christmas trees after all. However, just as you'd hoped, in four more years you'll have to crane your neck to see the neighbor's light.

The first word people intone when you tell them you're moving to the country is *garden*. They get all misty-eyed about dirt under the fingernails and sun on the back, and they suppose a garden will save them a good deal of money to boot. Actually, it will save very little money and cost a great deal of time. What we *can* grow without too much effort, after rocks (which heave up faithfully year after year), are zucchini and tomatoes. But then, anybody can grow zucchini and tomatoes, and everyone does. Zucchinis the size of newborns have been left on people's doorsteps in the dark of night. The Acme, too, can supply zucchini and tomatoes, and during the summer, zucchini and tomatoes, like all other vegetables which may be a bit more difficult to grow, are at their most plentiful and inexpensive. Besides, vegetable stands abound on country roads. With the rototiller, the lime, the time it takes to transport the manure from barn to garden— not to mention time spent maintaining the livestock that produces the manure—plus the endless weeding, it just plain *costs* money to have a garden if one's own time is worth anything at all. My advice: Buy your vegetables at the roadside stand and get a job.

Same with chicken. I was not a vegetarian when we moved here. We didn't eat a lot of meat, but a chicken or two now and then wasn't too great a moral infraction or health risk, we figured. (Part of the reason why many people eschew red meat but gobble up white meat has less to do with philosophy than with large soulful brown eyes versus little beady black ones.)

The books I'd read on self-sufficiency spoke warmly about the sense of continuity we'd feel with all of life if we raised and killed our own meat—you know, assumed our place in the ecological chain, albeit the link with the greatest advantage, as no one eats humans, so far. We dismissed pigs because of the high fat content, and couldn't conceive of how two people could eat that much bacon, anyway. We thought we'd start with a chicken—a manageable meal for two. I was a fowl-eating city girl on her way to becoming spiritually connected to all of life through a blood ritual with something that would offer up its very soul to me. I was going to learn to kill a chicken.

I asked the neighbors for advice. Now, folks in the sticks don't see many people from day to day, so they welcome a chance to chat about themselves and give advice on how to kill a chicken—or on any other subject, for that matter, so long as they get to be the expert. You have to listen to some pretty lengthy lectures in which your college degrees will be disparaged and your lack of practical knowledge emphasized. Your role is to shrug apologetically every so often and appear impressed. So there you are with night drawing down, standing around in the cold yard, wearing down a patch of your own grass by rubbing it over and over with the toe of your boot. But don't invite them in or you'll lose the advantage of the dwindling temperature as your only excuse to get on with your evening.

Here's their advice on killing a chicken: Build a box with a head hole in it. (Now, you just wanted chicken for dinner, not a big production, although it's finally dawning on you that everything you do yourself in the country is a big production.) Put the box over the chicken. The chicken is supposed to stick its head out of the hole, at which point, you're supposed to chop it off. (What's to keep the chicken from retracting its head when it sees you coming with the hatchet? Don't ask, if you want to get on with this project before dark.)

This method seemed laborious and a bit chancy, so I called our neighbor Sal, a Christian fundamentalist who lives over the hill in a panel truck outfitted with a bed and a tiny combination sink/stove/refrigerator. Sal lives a minimalist existence, but he does like his protein in the form of chicken, rabbits, turkeys, cows, and goats rather than something that dies a less colorful death like, say, beans.

Sal, a man of few words unless they're God's words, came over. No box with head-hole for him; he had another method in mind. He picked one of our chickens from her roost. (To capture a chicken you have to wait until it goes home for the night, around 4 p.m., and is snuggled down on its roost, which is just a stick across the width of the coop, several feet off the ground. You'll never catch one running after it in the yard. But you knew that.)

The method Sal was trying at the moment was to grab the chicken by the legs, fasten them together with baling twine, and hang the chicken upside down from a nail on the side of the barn. Then, with a sharp, narrow knife blade inserted into its mouth, he tried to cut the cords at the back of the chicken's throat. The chicken, obligingly screaming for its life, had its mouth open all right, but Sal couldn't reach in far enough. The opening was just too narrow, although Sal caused a lot of pain and loss of blood trying. Down came the chicken and I took over.

Frantic by now and sobbing apologies to the chicken, I placed its squirming body on a nearby log stump and began to mash what must have been a dull hatchet blade into the chicken's neck. I hacked and I sobbed, and eventually the chicken gave up the ghost and I gave up the whole dirty business of killing chickens and have eaten beans ever since.

One Saturday, we went to our first, and last, auction. In the local Pennysaver, I read that beehives were included among other items in the sale. We'd been giving some thought to getting bees for honey for ourselves and, in the back of our minds, hoping to supply the two health food stores in Binghamton. This turned out to be another of my fanciful notions about country living. Health food stores want a ready and plentiful supply of honey, not a few jars here and there as we could provide it. People who make a living from keeping bees do pretty much just that, not that in addition to another career, and it is a very hard life which results in a very small profit. The simple life may be one that is stripped of inessentials, but it is not an idle one.

During the first half of the sale, we watched faces, got our bearings, and refrained from bidding until the auctioneer pointed to the hives. I jumped in. There were nine hives, including bees. The auctioneer started the bidding at $10 per hive, for one or for all the hives, I understood him to say. I raised my hand and soon won out over the other bidder at $25. When the auctioneer asked if I wanted all nine hives, I said, "Why yes," thinking that it was one hive for $25 or *all* hives for $25. After all, we're just talking about wooden boxes with tiny buzzing insects! Believing we were started in the bee business for a mere $25, I jumped up and threw my arms around the seller's neck. When I got to the cashier, however, and she rang up $225, I saw what a fool I'd been. I wrote out a check for $225, hoping that the flourish with which I signed my name distracted onlookers from my inflamed cheeks.

We were to pick up the bees in the spring, after they'd wintered with their owner but, early in November, the beekeeper called to say that the bees were starving and we should pick them up immediately. We learned later they were starving because he'd sold off all the honey that would have fed them through the winter. Alarmed and entirely unarmed, we borrowed our neighbor Sal and his pickup truck and went over for the first load one evening, just before dark. We had no idea we were supposed to move very, very slowly around bees. In fact, we didn't know *anything* about bees. We must have entered the yard too enthusiastically, alarming the bees, which *were* armed in addition to being starving! They attacked, swarming up under our shirt sleeves, our pant legs, and getting snarled in my hair, which I'd foolishly worn down. They stung and stung us as we ran about like dervishes, slapping ourselves and each other as if we were on fire.

As we beat a hasty retreat from the bee yard, resolving to come back with the proper equipment, we looked up at the house and saw the owner's face in the window. Now that we'd paid him, he apparently felt no obligation to make good on his offer at the auction to help us load the hives into the truck.

On the drive home, Henderson and Sal said their pain was easing, but my face felt alive with red-hot needles. I didn't think I'd be able to sleep that night. I thought I should see what the hospital could do, so H and I said goodnight to Sal and drove to the emergency room of Barnes-Kasson Hospital in Susquehanna. The doctor on duty peered at my cheeks.

I thought he would find my condition as curious as we did, but he examined me with such coolness that I wondered if he'd just been reading up on bees moments before our arrival. He told us bee stings were common in a country ER and went on to list other types of injuries he regularly saw: gashes from chainsaws, limbs crushed by toppling tractors, and teenagers with head injuries from four-wheeler crashes. Then, one after the other, he picked from my face a total of seventeen stingers.

Wiser now, and determined not to lose the money we'd spent on these bees, we invested more. We bought two suits of beekeeping getup and hired an experienced beekeeper and his truck for the second trip. Now, looking like astronauts in stiff white coveralls, hats with facemasks and visors, and elbow-high gloves, we moved into the bee yard in exaggerated slow motion. The beekeeper, wearing none of the above, had brought with him a metal smoker. He lit a pine bob in the container, blew out the flame, and pumped on a rubber ball, causing smoke to issue forth. The smoke was supposed to pacify the bees when waved in their direction. It did. The bees buzzed gently around us in the night air.

We taped the three-tiered boxes together and secured them with shock cords to the bed of the truck. It took two trips to move the swarming hives in his rickety pickup from Montrose to our hillside, 20 miles east. We gingerly unloaded the heavy boxes in our driveway and carried them up to our orchard where, we hoped, the bees would fertilize the apple trees.

During this five-hour operation, the beekeeper was bitten only once, on his finger, despite dozens of bees swarming all over his hands and between his fingers. Moving extremely slowly is the key with bees. Another lesson in patience, plus a reminder of the advisability of being a trifle better informed at the start of a new venture. Nine beehives now sat in our orchard. On the beekeeper's advice, we made sugar-water feeders to replace their honey. These were jars with tiny holes punched in the lids, which we inverted over the top tier of the beehives. The bees could come up through a hole below and stick their tongues through the lid holes to feed. We protected the jars by building additional boxes that sat on top of each hive, making them now four tiers high. Week after week, we hauled on our astronaut gear and plowed through the snow up to the hives with bottles of sugar-water to feed the bees through the winter. But by spring, all the bees in all the hives were dead. Once again, our lonely little trial was mirrored on the entire East Coast: Many professional beekeepers lost up to one-third of their hives during one of the coldest winters ever.

There is a joke among confirmed beekeepers—and there *are* such people, who actually enjoy working with bees—that if given a million dollars, they would raise bees until they ran out of money.

As we never developed even a mild affection for bees, we gladly absorbed our losses, gave the lifeless hives and all our gear to Sal, and acquired some animals we could actually cuddle and in whose presence I find myself awash in a blissful reverie that may be as close to enlightenment as I'll ever come. Goats.

LEARNING FROM GOATS

...a symbiotic relationship with ruminants opens an
unguarded back gate to Eden...

Jim Corbett, *Goatwalking*

When I was a kid, my mother was so busy and so often harried I thought she didn't love me. Sometimes I used to feign illness in order to be permitted to stay home from grade school. I thought, what if Mother looks up from her housework on this particular day and turns, lovingly, in my direction between the hours of 8 a.m. and 3 p.m., but I am in school?

As a rebellious, sexually adventurous teenager, I got Mother's attention, all right. But finally I gave up the struggle and became just like her, so for many years now, I've had the inner satisfaction of knowing Mother would approve of my incessant busyness.

You'd be amazed what I can accomplish before 9 a.m. on an average day. You'll never find me just sitting around. I am constitutionally unable to watch daytime TV; I'm not even sure it's okay to watch TV at night. My daughter and my sister, independent of one another, each gave me a copy of *Meditations for Women Who Do Too Much* by Anne Wilson Schaef. Naturally I haven't made the time to read it straight through. God forbid Mother or I ever simply stopped, sat down, and, for a moment, accomplished nothing. Some urge from within that was not on our daily to-do list might well up—or, worse, nothing might. How would we know we existed? To be on the safe side, we never sat down.

I married, completed college, began a career as an alcoholism counselor, attended graduate school at night, maintained a home, and raised a child. When Mother thought my daughter needed a sibling, she suggested that if it were another girl I name her Belinda. But instead, my husband and I divorced, and I had my tubes tied. It wasn't until many years later, when my new husband, Henderson, and I moved to a farm in northeast Pennsylvania, that we were given two baby goats, and I had the opportunity to name my first kid Belinda.

Mother, who has been dead for 21 years now, would have liked Belinda. They are really very similar—both ladies, both thin and fastidious about their appearance. Mother never wore slacks in her entire life; Belinda, for her part, finds it unpleasant to step into water. Both have long, thin noses. And an expression of disdain finds their faces a congenial surface upon which to reside.

But of Belinda's love I am certain; she's never too distracted for affection. She discreetly positions herself next to me whenever possible. I can comb her endlessly, although she's not fond of rough-housing. She'll step aside and wait for me to calm down or transfer my exuberance to her big brother, Capricorn, a gentle, somewhat bewildered buck. Like all the goats, Capricorn is mesmerized by my stroking. He sways slightly in a trance. If I stop, he takes his big front hoof and paws at me till I continue. He is a big boy, and this sometimes results in bruises. It's best to keep on stroking or get up and call it a day.

I name these goats, nickname them, and then re-nickname them with names that play upon their original nicknames. While one doesn't take too many liberties with Belinda's name—Linda B'Linda or just a backward Linda-B—Capricorn doesn't seem to mind Corny Two Shoes or Sweet Corn at all.

For a few years, Capricorn impregnated Belinda each fall when she came into heat, and the dear girl produced, for our amazement and delight, dancing baby twins each spring. We kept the first generation, born the following year, and named them Ivy, as in "little lambsy divy" and GG, for Gray Goat, a takeoff on the name we gave our farmhouse when we first saw it in 1985, the Gray Ghost.

The gestation period for goats is five months. They go into heat in the fall and are supposed to give birth in the spring. But because our girls have always bedded down right beside their buck and therefore get pregnant as soon as the first heat is upon them, "spring" births always seem to land during a bitterly cold week in February. One baby was even born on a cold night before Christmas. We called him Billy Bejinks because Mother used to say the weather was "as cold as Billy Bejinks." I don't know who Billy Bejinks was or where the expression came from, but my daughter and her husband have further edited it. When they're shivering, it's "coooold as Billy!"

Capricorn knocked up his daughters Ivy and GG when they came of age. I'd read in my goat books that incest is okay as an animal husbandry technique to encourage desirable traits. With us, it was not for genetics but on account of what we saw as the friendliness of keeping all the animals together, and because of the impossibility of housing a pawing, moaning, thrashing male goat apart from the objects of his desire. However, after a dozen or so offspring we decided to bring in a new stud just to keep things on the up and up.

We sold as pets all the baby goats that were born after GG and Ivy, but we enjoyed the privilege of spending two early spring months with each set of newborns, the only creatures I know of who literally jump for joy when they're only two or three days old. Apart from watching them prance sideways down the hill when they are a week old and able to join the others on our daily walks, there is nothing more delicious than cuddling on one's lap a ribcage as thin and fluttery as a bird's, tucking the tired legs up under its soft furry little body, and kissing the face of a dozing baby goat.

Henderson and I resist using the proper names for the animals we've met in the country. It would sound pretentious and formal for me to call Belinda a doe and Capricorn a buck and the kids, kids. A bitch is an awful name for a female dog. So a cow is a cow, as is everything else out there in the farmer's field, male or female. (I've been told but I keep forgetting what a heifer is, and a steer. I believe these names refer to the state of the animal's reproductive organs; either she has not yet become pregnant or he has had his testicles lopped off so as not to get her pregnant.) In my lexicon, it's all very simple; boy animals are boys and girl animals are girls. But I suppose my anthropomorphizing might amuse the local farmers, who rightly look upon their barn inventory somewhat less fatuously.

The only goat we actually bought was Sweet William, a purebred Alpine, to be the new husband of our girls so we didn't carry this incest thing too far. We bought him from a neighbor farmer whose name was Bill, and as I was considering wildflowers as a category of future names and boy goats are called billys, I thought this name apt. However, it was a pretty limp-wristed name for the buck who was to be our main stud for the next four years.

He was the first and only goat we imported, and we found ourselves shocked and cringing at the bad luck that befell him once Belinda perceived him to be a threat to her girls, who, like him, were adolescents. Belinda, the light of Sweet William's eyes, the replacement for the mother he'd just lost, his future bride, tried to break Sweet William's bones. Sweet would moon around after Belinda from a distance, hoping she'd notice him. She noticed him all right and charged, again and again, bashing him sideways against the wire fence so hard we heard the reverberation at the house. She'd swivel, rear up, and charge again. She was possessed with the idea that Sweet William should die right there in the goat yard. All he wanted was her love.

Finally, as he inevitably gained on her in size, her will to kill him flagged, and miraculously, that fall she let him mount her. They've been inseparable companions since. (However, I do not think we can extrapolate from this any parallel to human male-female relations.)

We had to castrate Capricorn because Sweet William, younger, bigger, and now the herd queen's main squeeze, tried to eradicate him. Once again the sounds of foreheads thudding together rose to the house, and appalled, we watched as they even drew blood.

The vet came one late spring day and tranquilized a humbled Capricorn, who stood, legs apart and swaying, while the vet injected Novocain into the testicle area and, when it had taken effect, sliced down both scrota to expose what looked like huge veined eyeballs. He gathered the two eyeballs in his left hand, pulled them down firmly, and sliced through the cords with which they were attached to the body. I don't remember much blood. Then he sliced off the bottoms of the now empty scrotum, left them unstitched, and when they healed they just hung there, tiny reminders of Corn's former prowess. For several days afterward Capricorn walked gingerly, his back legs slightly apart.

I may resist using the proper nouns for livestock, but I'm enough of a farm girl to appreciate an opportunity to recycle. I threw the dogs one testicle each and watched, intrigued, as they chewed them right up.

From the coupling of Sweet William and GG came Daisy, whom we nicknamed Daisy-May (and Daisy-May-And-Then-Again-She-May-*Not*). She was an exceptionally affectionate little goat, and Henderson relented and said we could keep her. The next year, all four girls delivered babies; all the babies went to good homes. But now I began to feel that allowing our girls to become pregnant year after year might not be good for their bodies, and I suspected that, even with my head-over-heels amore for those of the caprine persuasion, the goat population of Susquehanna County would eventually peak, the pet market would be saturated, and we'd be trucking the babies to auction just prior to Easter and Passover; they'd be bought by Greeks and Jews, we were told, and eaten as the holiday treat, chevron. This time Sweet William stood legs apart, trembled, and walked gingerly for several post-op days.

Mating season, while offspringless, occurs each month now. The girls go into heat, and Capricorn is best advised to show no interest. Sweet William's still herd buck and spends his days in a miserable frenzy sniffing the girls' bottoms, hanging his mouth under their stream of urine, lifting his head, pulling back his upper lip so it comes closer to his nostrils to better smell the odor of the urine—and then suddenly, out of the corner of one eye, he takes notice of poor, innocently-standing-by Capricorn, who gets charged and flattened.

On one winter walk, Sweet was busy sniffing and empty-humping his girls, and Capricorn, although minding his own business, must still have seemed like a threat. I was walking ahead, goatherd, minding my own business, too, when Sweet charged Corn, who bolted, looked back in surprise at Sweet, and without watching where he was going, charged right into me. My legs flew straight up, at right angles to my body. I hung a few seconds in midair before landing, sharply, on my bottom in the snow. The blow floored me, knocking my teeth together, immediately banging out a headache, hurting my feelings unreasonably, embarrassing me, and causing me to look around nervously to see if my awkward mishap there in the woods had been spotted. Of course we were quite alone, and the heartless goats, used to blows of this sort, ignored me and kept on cramming white pine needles down their throats as fast as their smug, lipless lips could work.

Out of all this coupling, productive and non, out of all the hours feeding and milking goats in the barn and making cheese seven months out of every year, and just before SW gave up his balls, came the best-loved little goat princess ever born at Gray Ghost Farm, my own bottle-fed, breast-fed if I could have, lovingly hand-nursed four then two then one and now, sadly, no times a day, my own last-of-the-lot, light-of-my-life, Rosemary. I was considering herbs as a name category when she was born. Her brother, whom the mother, Miss Ivy, did *not* leave to wither, the fat, warm, well-licked Basil, eventually went to auction. Rosemary came to bed with me.

What else could I do? We checked the barn as soon as we got home from Cape May after my daughter's twenty-nineth birthday and found Basil doing well beside his bemused mother. But off near the milk stand, squished against the cold wall of the shed, was a wet and trembling jumble of bones, and it was a girl. Girls are more desirable because they give milk, obviously, don't become as big as boys, and don't pee straight into their own mouths if the opposite sex is near and in heat. Besides, I like a goat in bed with me, under the electric blanket.

I put down a towel, naturally, should she pee, but with death on its way, all systems are down and you have to worry first about cold, and then something to put into the little body before something can come out. I'd read goat books, which served mostly to terrify me into assisting at births when I really wasn't needed, but because of their advice, I'd frozen some of last year's colostrum. We thawed it and, with a large plastic syringe, squirted tiny amounts between Rosie's locked jaws. She'd given up hope and was calling it a rather cold and unenviable day. We weren't.

We got her to agree with us. We took her out of my bed (if we were lucky, her little system eventually would work) and placed her on a towel on an electric heating pad with a moisture-proof cover in a big cardboard box at the foot. During the day, we moved her in her box to the shop where I work so I could cuddle her on my lap. She gathered strength as I forced more and more colostrum down her throat. Eventually, I substituted the colostrum with milk from her mom. Finally, she agreed to suck. Then suddenly, she sucked with such certainty she swept the bottle out of my hand!

By the second day she was standing. By the third, standing and walking were easy. By the fourth night, when we went to bed at 10 p.m., Rosie in her box, I in my bed, Rosie stood right up, head tilted smartly over the side of the box, indicating she was ready to play. I called Henderson. "I don't think Rosie's a house goat any more." He took her to the barn. My sleep matters to me.

Of course she bellowed, but somehow she managed to find enough warmth among the others to get through the night. Her mother never has recognized her, and I am proud to be the only mother Rosie's ever known.

I am unabashedly head-over-heels in love with goats—but about Rosemary in particular I am rhapsodic. In the barn, it's Rosemary May and Rosie May and Rosie Pay and Rosie Posie Mosie Dosie Bosie May until I nauseate even myself. We have a hugging and kissing bee each morning after I milk. Rosie, now a chunky one-year-old adolescent, jumps up on top of the feed bin and leans forward, all in one motion, against my body which is right there, arms open to gather her in. She licks the salt off my neck and cheeks, and I pummel and scratch her and gather up her thick skin and hair in folds and look for the itches that all goats have along their sides and backs and that they can't reach with their teeth. When I do her armpits, her licking tapers off as she concentrates on the pleasure, her amber eyes close to slits, and she leans into my chest for balance so that if I stepped backward suddenly, which I never would, she'd topple.

I kiss goats on the mouth. Occasionally I get mouth sores that Henderson says is from kissing goats. Then he says I have goatitis. I don't care. I'm intrigued by their mumble mouths, lipless mouths, like llamas. They have only bottom teeth in the front. Top and bottom in the back, for grinding, but only bottom ones in the front and smooth gums like a baby on top. They only need bottom ones for biting off leaves and bark.

In my work with alcoholics in Philadelphia, I knew men without top or bottom teeth, all pulled by the welfare system, which figured one dentist visit once and for all is economically prudent. I have secretly recoiled from the toothless mouth. Now I have been right up in that toothlessness looking for the cud, and on goats, toothlessness is a most charming and sensible dental arrangement. I am gaga over goats.

I keep trying to catch a glimpse of their cud but so far haven't been able to. I'm fascinated by their cud—or rather, what I'm really fascinated by is a creature that thinks to chew its food again, being a bolter of food myself who scarcely chews it the first time. I cannot imagine a life placid enough to chew my food twice. I get the food in as fast as possible, as much as possible in one sitting, and I'm off. Ruminants teach me about patience; even their digestive process calls for it.

Like cows and sheep, goats have a four-chambered digestive system. The largest chamber is the *rumen*. Here, grain and grass get churned and fermented into four to five gallons of liquid—fatty acids, protein, amino acids, and vitamins. Any large, coarse material that doesn't succumb to the churning is sent back to the goat's mouth for further chewing. This is the cud. The *reticulum* pumps the fermented fluid to the *omassum*, a structure consisting of folds of tissue for increased surface and, therefore, better absorption. The *abomassum* is the true stomach where actual digestion occurs, where protein is broken down into easily absorbed simple compounds. The end product of a goat's digestive tract is a gentle trickle of pellets—small, oval, odorless, and perfectly packaged.

Together, Belinda and I learned to milk. Now I'm a pro. I sit down right next to each goat on the milk stand, my cheek against her side, her sweet hay smell in my nostrils, and reach under with soap and a warm washcloth and clean her udder. She's having her grain. I squeeze her teat just so and squirt milk into the container. But doing four goats takes so long I need to listen to books on tape or time my milking to correspond with *All Things Considered* on public radio not to be bored. I am not, as you see, a meditator.

My daughter found a book for me called *Goatwalking*. She inscribed it "For my Mother, the goat." The author, Jim Corbett, understands why being with goats frees one from responsibility for carrying the relationship, which humans do with dogs, for instance. "Unlike pets, goats never seem to think they're human, but they tolerate physical differences and allow properly behaved human beings to become fully accepted members of the herd." It is my wish to become so properly behaved. Under a section titled "Doing Nothing,"

Corbett writes: "Being useless uncovers despair," and his discovery exposes my compulsive need to be busy.

I moved to this farm 12 years ago, tired and close to an edge. For years I have held up the earth with my shoulders, and I've had the migraines to prove it. It's been my job to see that between friends there are no misunderstandings. I am the cause of a party's failure (and its success as well, I might add). I am the cause of the automobile breaking down, the source of any pain in my relationship with my daughter. I longed to live close to things that were beyond my domination, beyond even the thought of domination, things that could get along without me, like mountains and trees. Like goats.

During the long hours of the day when I'm inside working, the goats are getting along fine without me. I gaze at them through the window. They're all chewing their cud or peeing, often simultaneously. They doze, heads hanging. They are caught in the moments of their lives as I am never able to be. Like the mountains around them, they are implacable, steadfast, steady, and present. They have something eternal running through them that is not of my making or my maintaining. That is a big relief.

Goats are concentrating, unconsciously, on the flavor of the grain, the saliva in their mouths, the grinding of their stomachs, and the returning of the cud. They are certainly not accomplishing anything. They are, let's face it, grand meditators, and that's what I want to learn from them. To learn to focus, to concentrate so narrowly I forget myself in the moment and am unself-conscious.

I always resolve to stay longer in the barn, brushing the goats. But it's too close to not getting anything accomplished and I'm up and off, promising to spend more time tomorrow. Yet, when I can pull myself down, sit down on the milk stand with wire brush in hand, all are takers. They gently offer me their noses and throats and press against each other to get closer to my hand. Seven big bodies jockeying to be groomed—Belinda and Capricorn and Sweet William and their children Ivy, GG, Daisy, and Rosemary. All my children, too. This press of life catches me up in its immediacy and I am lost for just a minute in getting my hands and forearms and elbows to touch each warm, breathing, beloved body in as many places as I can reach and kissing as many cheeks and noses and yes oh yes lips as I can and being as much a goat myself as I can be.

I still haven't spent a day or even a few hours up on the hillside, in a chair, with the goats, even with some distraction like books to ward off the demons of uselessness that arise from my central fear that if I quiet down too much I'll find I don't exist at all.

This summer, however, I might chance it.

LIVING HIGH ON THE HILL

We were broke. We'd poured all our money into rebuilding the nineteenth-century farmhouse we purchased in 1985. The attempts we made to achieve self-sufficiency from the 71 acres of land that came with it were largely unsuccessful. We had examined our 50-acre wood lot with an eye to a lumber sale. We'd planted Christmas trees. We'd raised chickens and slaughtered one. We'd pressed our own apples for cider, planted a vegetable garden, invested in honeybees, and invited a local farmer to hay our fields for what we hoped would be enough money to pay our real estate taxes. We raised goats, sold some of the kids, kept seven adults, learned to milk them and to make goat cheese.

However, the timber wasn't mature enough to sell; the Christmas trees, ditto. We were squeamish about slaughter, exhausted by the apple pressing, and stung by the bees. Only the goats were a delight, though nothing more than a hobby, and the hay the farmer cut went to feed them, not pay our taxes.

In place of these impractical ideas, I could imagine at first only the alternatives of waitressing and real estate. I'd been an associate real estate broker in my Philadelphia incarnation, and I spent a few seasons in Susquehanna county selling real estate until the market soured. As for waitressing, I'd never make ends meet in a county where, when a husband wanted to show extra appreciation for my service, he'd drop another 50 cents into my hand behind his wife's back, with a conspiratorial wink. Henderson found a factory job, which, bless his heart, he's still at, uncomplainingly, 15 years later.

Finally I conceived of a plan to open a health food shop in our home—at first to sell beans and grains to the few vegetarians residing in this dairy-drinking, meat-eating county, and then to the rest of the world, via mail order. I'd call it Heartland Foods. (Admittedly, northeast Pennsylvania is far from the heartland of America, but it is the land where my heart lies, and I had admired the movie *Heartland*.)

Our health food delivery service appealed to the kind of local people we'd met during community rallies to keep abortion legal, the same people who started a branch of the League of Women Voters, made up the membership of the local artists guild, and either struggled to eke out an alternative lifestyle as musicians-turned-carpenters or had arrived here from Philadelphia and New York City financially independent.

An advertisement in *Vegetarian Times* brought me customers from places as distant and exotic as Sicily, Japan, Germany, and Tbilisi—from folks in the U.S. Army living overseas with nary a granule of whole grain nor a sliver of Soysage to fill their bellies. One display ad cost $600 and brought an onslaught of requests for our free catalog, though most queries never resulted in a sale—a predicament I understand is typical in the mail order biz.

Still, in my optimism, I imagined that all those requests for the free catalog warranted taking out another mortgage on our house to build a large addition for the store. With generous gifts from family and large Visa loans, I purchased a photocopier (on which to Xerox the nine-page quarterly catalog), a second refrigerator, a chest freezer, shelving along three of the four walls, a desk, and a computer. For seven years, the health food business kept me off the streets and made me feel, in spite of scant pecuniary evidence, that having a job to show up at each day meant I was providing a useful service. The money would follow.

What is it that successful businesspeople know that I don't? Did I seek advice from the Small Business Administration? Yes I did. Three-piece-suited elderly men found their way up the dirt road to our store and spent several hours boasting about their own former successes as widget salesmen, but either I wasn't paying attention or they neglected to offer any tips to help me earn my first million. Two MBA students from Binghamton University came for a semester of Wednesday afternoons to analyze my business. Again, if they suggested anything to help me earn even my first $100,000, it sailed right over my head. Finally, I hired a consultant from Binghamton, a guy who flirted with me, which was okay, but who offered little applicable advice, which wasn't. In doing the figures, he failed to take into account the cost of advertising—that is, how much tofu I'd have to sell to make back the money spent on advertising and whether or not one person could actually box up and ship out that much tofu without hiring a helper whose salary, in turn, would eat into the profits.

I admit I've never been much interested in making money. I've always worked, mind you, but never made enough to ice the cake. In recent years, my father has taken pity on me, and now a monthly check goes out to each of his three daughters. It is not a sum large enough to live on, but it enables me to make stabs at unsuccessful ventures.

We muddled along. Four years into the mail-order/delivery business, I found I was efficient enough at running it to look up from my desk one day and propose to Henderson that we share the beauty of our place with others by setting ourselves up as a guesthouse. Our local diner and family restaurant are dismal places, so we'd offer three meals a day. Henderson said, as he has to all my other ideas, "Go for it."

Helpless to know where else to turn for advice, I called on the same business consultant I'd hired when starting up Heartland Foods. What I'd found to be true for that business was also true for the Gray Ghost Guesthouse: Advertising to reach potential guests was more costly than I could ever earn back in overnight stays, especially as we could handle only one set of guests per weekend.

This time, the business consultant lost me as a client by offering decidedly bad advice. He must have been of the opinion that city folks who needed a weekend break from their high-pressure jobs, were, during their off hours, idiots. He suggested that for a weekend stay I charge the astronomical price of $500. He was confident that folks would thrill to the idea of petting our goats (we had seven by then), delight in hiking the logging trails that weave through our woods, and relish the three gourmet meals. Plus, two days spent in the company of one of the unlikeliest couples they would ever meet would be worth every penny.

He did add (parenthetically) that if, when it came to settling their tab, the guests protested they'd been overcharged—comparing the amount of pleasure they'd received to the amount of money they'd paid—I could always agreeably dash them off a refund check for half the amount.

I learned this: People who can afford a $500 weekend jaunt from New York City or Philadelphia to rural Pennsylvania (where the toothlessness of the citizenry is eclipsed only by its obesity) already have a weekend retreat in the Poconos. For those who can't and don't, even $250 was extortionate.

Now, three years later, you can stay at our guesthouse and have a bedroom with hall bath and breakfast for $75 per couple. Mind you, we'll probably join you for breakfast, which you'll eat in our kitchen— a large, sun-filled room, to be sure, with a genuine barn beam supporting the ceiling and held up by a hand-hewn post in the middle of the floor—but a kitchen, nonetheless, not a formal dining room with pewter serving dishes and an antique sideboard. For $120 per couple, it's bed, breakfast, lunch, champagne, and a three-course evening repast made according to your specific dietary requirements. All our guests have taken us up on the full treatment.

I wrote the copy for the brochure about our place, describing the quiet and emphasizing its rustic nature—just plywood sub-flooring in the living rooms until we can afford to lay down random-width pine. Prospective guests should expect long walks and bonfires instead of four-posters and Victoriana. We had a photo of us taken for the brochure to show guests that Henderson and I are black and white, respectively. I advertised, sent out the brochures, and over the last several summers we've entertained eight couples. This was hardly a get-rich-quick (or *ever*) scheme, but we've enjoyed sharing the beauty of our place, and each visit has provided us with congenial company and piquant anecdotes.

Preparing and presenting sumptuous gourmet meals and making conversation are not Henderson's strong suits, so the running of the guesthouse falls to me. During the week prior to a guest weekend, one piece of my brain pulses with migraine. Even though our guests have pre-screened themselves—we get only nonprejudiced, athletic folks who like dogs and goats—I worry how Henderson and I will appear to them. I majored in English and psychology at college and recently completed a master's degree. Henderson dropped out of school in the ninth grade at age 16.

Sometimes Henderson stammers and garbles his words, and I worry that guests will privately make fun of his mispronunciations. I worry every bit as much that I'll reveal an unflattering characteristic, talk too much, or ask a second time something a guest has already answered, like how long it took them to get to the farm, showing that earlier I wasn't paying any attention whatsoever. Having guests requires a performance, and somewhere deep inside I cower during the entire weekend they're here, expecting to be exposed at any moment as anything but the gracious, self-confident hostess I'm impersonating. I'm a pretty good actress, I guess, who appears to have everything under control, but knowing that's the impression I give doesn't reduce my anxiety over a possible slip.

Henderson and I are at our best when the focus is off us—when we're hiking, for instance—and guests seen equally happy to have us escort them along the logging roads that lace through our forest. We've even developed a system. After they've changed their clothes, the guests and I set out on a walk through the woods to Hawkins Pond and the big bluestone quarry over the hill about two miles from our house, accompanied by our four bounding, barking, no-breed country dogs. Eventually, the dogs will "thin out," as Henderson says, noses to the ground, ears flattened against heads, hightailing it after the local fauna. The walk is strenuous enough to be called a hike—all uphill on the outward leg, through leafy woods with occasional clearings and green vistas.

Meanwhile, Henderson will put two bottles of champagne on ice in a backpack and set off up the other side of the mountain with the goats. They'll hike up to what we call the roundabout—a big circle of grass I mow halfway up our mountain—a spot with a fine vista of the undulating Endless Mountains, a wooden love seat to view them from, a fire pit, and several wobbly lawn chairs, off one of which a certain guest, after a third glass of champagne, slowly toppled, giggling and unharmed. There, Henderson will unload the chilled bubbly and continue up the mountain, followed by the faithful goats.

By that time, the guests and I will have covered about a mile and a half around the other side of the mountain. All of a sudden, out of the silence of the woods ahead comes a Tarzan call—a Aah, a Aah—which I answer, Jane-like—A ah, A ah—jungle-calling to Henderson to the amusement of the guests. Around the bend come seven large black/gray/white/tan goats, prancing stiff-legged down the path toward us, blatting inquisitively. Henderson, leaning on the long staff of a goatherd, is grinning in their midst. This moment alone might be worth $500 in some absolute sense, especially to city people more accustomed on their downtown strolls to surprises of the attempted-mugging variety or near-death experiences with speeding cabbies.

The 15 of us (humans, goats, and the slavering dogs, who've rejoined us) continue on to Hawkins Pond or hike up to marvel at the view from the edge of the quarry, then tramp back to the roundabout, where the humans will down the champagne, watch the sun set, and trundle down the path to the house for dinner. The meal itself is accompanied by all the beer and wine the guests desire and that my nerves require as long as I can still perform upright. Lube 'em up with alcohol and they'll pay no attention to the little person behind the curtain.

The next morning I arise early, dress myself in self-assurance, and organize breakfast:

Organic Coffee
Freshly Squeezed Orange Juice
Fruit Compote drizzled with Triple Sec
French Toast, the Egg whipped with Brandy and Orange Zest,
topped with Locally Tapped Maple Syrup.

The guests wander down around eight.

We are now recovering vegetarians, but in consideration for our mostly vegetarian guests, my menus are meatless. All of our guests read about us in the Heartland Foods catalog, except the couple I remember as the "candle guests," who were the winning bidders of our public radio station's annual fund-raising auction. I'd donated a weekend at the Gray Ghost Guesthouse to WSKG; Tom and B.J. came in with the highest bid.

Tom was a man in his late forties, with a graying ponytail. His wife, B.J., looked younger and was his opposite in every way observable. Her hair was professionally coifed and frosted, her eyebrows were arched and augmented, and her rouge and lipstick were freshly applied, probably in the car coming up our dusty road. Tom wore dungarees and a plaid shirt. B.J. wore a madras blouse and matching Bermuda shorts with determined front creases, white Keds, and those little half-socks with tassels in back. In their real lives, they owned a fully air-conditioned home near Cayuga Lake, where they docked their small yacht. The reason they wanted to leave what sounded like an ideal vacation spot for a weekend in the mountains was because Tom wanted to see our goats. B.J. wasn't particularly interested in them but came along anyway.

They arrived on July 14, 1995, which happened to be the hottest day of any year anyone could remember. Ordinarily, mountain weather can be awkward even in summer due to the number of times you have to take off clothes and put them back on over the course of one day. The temperature can rise 30 degrees between morning and noon, then fall so low again by bedtime that you need the electric blanket on under your quilt. Sorry to say, this day did not annoy us with temperature fluctuations—the thermometer needle never budged from 94 degrees, even at bedtime. Henderson and I had gotten along fine for ten years with only a small floor fan. He doesn't mind the heat and, on the few nights of the year that it was still hot when we went to bed, I'd wring out a washcloth in cold water and spread it out across my naked chest. With the fan blowing across me, this spot air-conditioning allowed me to drift off to sleep comfortably.

I'd taken the temperature into consideration when preparing dinner:

Chilled Curried Zucchini Soup

It slid down easily, cooled us, and was followed by

Caesar Salad.

Dessert, too, was cold:

Vanilla Ice Cream Parfaits in frosted glasses,
Laced with Frangelico or Kahlua

Only the entree was hot:

Seitan Bourguignonne on Organic Garlic/Parsley Fettuccini
(This meatless variation calls for pearl onions, fresh mushrooms, thyme, burgundy,
and seitan—a meat substitute made from chunks of wheat gluten, which, when
cooked and stained with the red wine, has the consistency and color of boeuf.)

We thought it was a delicious main course and assumed it was unusual, as well, but when I announced the entrée, B.J. said, "Oh, yes, I make that quite often."

Over dinner, Tom told us at some length about his meditation practices. B.J., very much a resident of this earthly plane, fanned herself, wiped perspiration from her upper lip, and murmured how awfully hot it was.

"Yes, *uncharacteristically* so!" I said, hoping to emphasize the capriciousness of nature and, thereby, our unaccountability. It was then that Tom and B.J. told us about the air-conditioning back home and the yacht, and with that, the odor of goat manure, which is ordinarily inoffensive, wafted in through the open kitchen windows, the screens of which failed also to prevent the occasional fly from getting in and dive-bombing the dinner plates as we ate.

We retired. I hoped they'd had enough champagne and wine with dinner to sleep through the night, but on the way up to bed, B.J. again complained of the heat, jokingly suggesting she could always spend the night at the local air-conditioned motel and come back for Tom in the morning. Tom laughed. He was a sport. He said he didn't think it was all that hot. Roughing it was what the experience was all about, after all. We set up our little fan in one of their windows and wished them a good night. I arranged my wet washcloth and drifted off.

At 1 a.m., I awoke to hear a car start up and pull out of the driveway. I thought, ah, so B.J.'s gone to spend the night at the motel; I turned over and went back to sleep.

In the morning, I tiptoed downstairs to begin breakfast, and when Henderson came down to help, I cautioned him to be quiet, certain that even if B.J. had gone to the motel (the car was indeed gone), Tom, our pony-tailed goat admirer, had stuck it out and was probably meditating in the living room. Henderson and I crept to the door of the living room and peered in. Empty. I thought, well, then, he's still in their bedroom, the door of which was closed. So at 9 a.m., I tiptoed up, rapped lightly on the door, and then gradually opened it upon another empty room. They had both fled in the night.

Later that morning, they called and left an apologetic message on our answering machine.

Later still, when I was tidying up the kitchen, I noticed that on the cookbook shelf behind my chair at the dining table, one of the two upright candles had melted into an upside-down *U*. Its wick was nearly touching the shelf. This meant that all during dinner, B.J., who had sat opposite me, fanning herself, had subliminally watched the candle slowly surrender to the heat. A night hot enough to melt wax was surely something to flee. We went out that morning and bought three large floor fans, which have lived in the closet 362 days out of every year since.

Our very first guests were Heartland Foods customers—Madeline and Mark, a copyeditor and a chemical engineer, respectively. Throughout my preparation of breakfast, lunch, and dinner (which, hell-bent as I seem to be on providing myself with opportunities for migraines, always includes at least one new recipe that I must closely read and follow without interruption), they sat at the kitchen table and talked to me. I answered as best I could and cooked as best I could, and apparently did both well enough for them to remain friends and Heartland Foods customers. I've since practiced that first dinner menu, and can now prepare it and talk (and chew gum) at the same time.

Swiss Chard Soup with Garlic and Hot Pepper Chips
Polenta Puttanesca
Asparagus with Browned Butter and Lemon Sauce
Bananas in Ginger Syrup
(Polenta is a cornmeal and Parmesan mush that you spread in the bottom of a glass pie pan
and smother with a "brazen" tomato, caper, and Kalamata olive sauce.
Puttanesca comes from the Italian puttana, which means whore.)

The next day, as they were leaving, Madeline looked up to the edge of our woods and pointed out a scarlet tanager. We stood and shared their binoculars with dropped jaws. It was the only time I'd ever seen one, before or since.

Carl and Kay spent a night that September. They were planning to convert their nineteenth-century home outside of Scranton into a bed-and-breakfast and were gathering data and researching the competition by sleeping around in a few B&Bs. I mildly resented that their visit stemmed from this ulterior motive, but in this I was admittedly irrational, as we had done the very same thing when starting up. They asked in advance that I serve no beets or cantaloupe, no Indian food or spices, and, if possible, no fat. Carl was a veterinarian (though not a vegetarian) and was trying to lose weight. Dinner was

Roasted Sweet Red Pepper Soup
(minus the optional dash of cayenne and with a mere comma of heavy cream floating in the middle)
Baked Salmon with a Lime-Chive (nonfat) Sour Cream Sauce on Wild Rice
Green Beans Amandine
Raspberry Sorbet with Kiwi Slices
(an elegant and entirely fat-free dessert)

The red pepper soup always gets raves. I serve it for almost every new set of guests. Without the called-for dollop of heavy cream, it is entirely vegan—simply a puree of roasted red peppers sautéed until soft in olive oil, with onions, lemon juice, and basil. Although it is tedious to sear and then, standing, peel the skins from the red peppers, the result is heavenly—a comfort food par excellence, except for the discomfort of preparing it. Everyone asks for the recipe but later admits it was too much trouble to actually make.

Marj and Phil are vegans who had been Heartland Foods customers for several years when they called to make reservations. She's a plastic surgeon; he's a real estate mogul. Phil's short and Jewish; Marj is tall and Irish, although after they married, she converted to Judaism and, in fact, has a small side practice as a mohel (a ritual circumcisor). Marj and I hit it off and talked nonstop; Phil and H piped up when they could wedge in a word.

Vegans are tricky to cook for. They eat no animal or insect products or byproducts. Think about it—that's no meat or fish, naturally, and no cheese, cream, or milk. No eggs, either, with which to bind the muffins (Egg Replacer is not quite as effective), and no honey with which to sweeten them. Vegans say that taking the extra honey from a beehive is insect exploitation.

I found vegan blueberry muffin and ginger cookie recipes which Marj and Phil thought were delicious, and I cobbled together what turned out to be a menu delectable and attractive enough to serve to anyone, vegan or not, beginning with my favorite stand-by, sans cream:

Roasted Sweet Red Pepper Soup
Zucchini Boats Stuffed with Smoked Eggplant and Ginger
Spicy Curried Chickpeas
Sliced Tomatoes Drizzled with Olive Oil and Chopped Fresh Basil
Apple Crisp Made from Our Own King Apples

When they got back to Brooklyn after their first weekend with us, Phil treated his partner and his wife to a fall weekend at the Ghost. The Wahalas were from Staten Island. They were young and athletic, and they spent all day Saturday hiking up Elk Mountain and so were blessedly gone for the entire day while, without interruption, I prepared their harvest dinner:

Creamy Butternut Squash Soup with Ginger, Leeks, and Apples
Patrani Machi
Jasmine Rice
Ben & Jerry's Coffee Ice Cream Sprinkled with
Ground Hazelnut Coffee Beans
(Patrani Machi is an Indian recipe for flounder with a coconut and ginger chutney
rolled in romaine leaves and drizzled with butter and lime juice)

John and Kathy are fly-fishing bikers (*mountain* bikers, that is) who arrived the same week I happened to be reading *A River Runs Through It*. While I still have no idea what mechanical engineers do (John and Kathy are both this thing), I was at least able to appreciate the difficulty of casting, which Norman Maclean so beautifully describes in the early pages of his book. John and Kathy spent the first day fishing on the Delaware River, returning for an Indian dinner:

Mixed Curried Vegetables on Organic White Basmati Rice
Lemon/Date Chutney, Peach Chutney
Banana Raita, Cucumber Raita
Toasted Cashews, Raisins, and Coconut Toppings
Red Lentil Dhall (a curried bean dish)

This is a delicious and visually dazzling menu, and, except for the raitas, which have a yogurt base, entirely vegan. One hardly needs dessert because of the sweet chutneys and tangy raitas, but I prepared it, just in case:

Almond Cheese Pie with Toasted Pine Nuts
(from our homemade goat ricotta)

Each set of guests has made their bed, kindly relieving me of that domestic chore, but when John and Kathy went fishing, I did run in and vacuum up a fearsome number of flies, which swarm on the inside of the screens when the weather turns cooler each fall.

On their second afternoon, John and Kathy asked us to show them the five-mile loop of dirt roads that surround our mountain. The route takes you into New York State, past Hawkins Pond, through a dark pine forest with row after row of hemlocks, pines, spruces, and firs planted some 30 years ago, and around by a modest cabin stuck back in the woods. Built on the iron I-beams that support a house-trailer, its one room is the width and length of a trailer, with a small screened porch addition. Here lives our neighbor Sal, a Christian fundamentalist we met the autumn we moved here. Over the years, Sal has supplied us with all our animals: twin baby goats, from which our herd of seven grew; a pair of rabbits, who were promptly eaten in the night; and, every ten years or so, a pair of puppies. I put my foot down at this last litter and urged him again to spay his female. But my words are wasted. Sal says the Bible calls for multiplying.

Ever since his heart attack at age 50, when Sal saw God, he's been on disability, a meager income that for a decade allowed him to live only in a panel truck on a piece of land lent to him by a local farmer.

A few years ago, he built the cabin on the same property. People from his church donated everything from carpentry help to roofing materials. We donated, among other things, nine beehives from our failed honey business. New York State pays his electricity bill, so while otherwise nearly penniless, Sal has a chest freezer someone gave him, which he stocks with meat. He buys baby turkeys and geese in the spring and lets them pluck nourishment from his yard until they're fat enough to slaughter. On the day we passed his house, there within the fence among the geese and turkeys was a sweet, brown-eyed calf whose name, Sal grinned, was T-bone.

Sal boasted that he had an entire bear in his freezer. Earlier that week, a big brown bear had been drawn to the beehives. The bear had taken a swipe at one of Sal's five tethered dogs, and when Sal tried to shoo him off, the bear rose up on his hind legs and waved his paws. Sal shot him in the heart. He skinned him, cut him up into dinner-sized pieces, and loaded him into his freezer. A single man whose boots are disintegrating around his toes and whose hand-me-down dungarees and work shirts are threadbare and stained, Sal has enough meat in his freezer to sustain for an entire winter all the families on one square block in the town of Susquehanna.

"How 'bout beans and rice, Sal," I weakly suggested at the end of his story, to which he smiled benignly at my ignorance and said, "The Bible tells us that animals were put on earth for our nourishment."

"Beans," I mumbled again to our guests as we pulled away from Sal's place and trudged toward home. We shook our heads and marveled at the arrogance that the original Bible scribes couldn't have known their words would inspire.

Two years after their first visit, Marj and Phil called to make a second reservation. Dinner the first night was:

Chilled Cucumber Soup with Basil and Dry Vermouth
West African Ground Nut Stew Garnished with
Pineapple Slices and Coconut
(zucchini, sweet potatoes, and green peppers sautéed with coriander and ginger
in a peanut butter sauce)
Whole Wheat Couscous
Blueberries and Kiwi Tossed with Raspberry Sorbet
Lace Oatmeal Cookies

The next morning, after a leisurely breakfast, Marj and Phil invited me and the dogs to join them for a walk. Henderson had to work that Saturday. As we were coming down the home stretch across the hayfield, we heard an odd, high-pitched cry. Repeated over and over, it sounded like the distressed call of a baby animal. We turned sharply in its direction and trooped through the tall grass toward the cries. As we got closer, we could see the four dogs circling something in the grass, wagging their tails. Closer still, we saw they were nosing a baby deer. It was on its side, struggling to rise to its feet, pawing the air with three legs, the fourth bloody and useless. I shooed away the dogs, stooped down, and gathered up the wriggling body, tucking the good legs under my arms. I turned and marched back across the meadow and down the hill toward the house, Marj and Phil and the (probably culprit) dogs following. Marj was in tears. She could see what I couldn't—the bad leg was hanging by only a shred of skin from the fawn's body.

As we walked, we planned our strategy. When we reached the house, Marj slid into the passenger seat of my car, took off her outer shirt, spread it across her lap, and reached up to receive the fawn. Phil and I put the dogs in the fenced-in yard, went into the house, and punched in the number for our vet. I thought he might be able to amputate the leg, and I pictured bringing the deer home, folding it into our existing menagerie, and sheltering it for life. But our vet said deer don't do well in captivity. (Pause.)

"Well, then, would you put him down?" I asked. He demurred. He said that wild animals come under the jurisdiction of the Game Commission. He could lose his license if he treated the deer.

He gave me the toll-free number for the Game Commission, and I called. Busy. Phil and I went outside to the car to report this to Marj and see how the fawn was holding up. It may have been in shock, for its cries came less often, but when they did, they were shrill and plaintive; its big brown eyes were liquid with fear.

Standing alongside the car, I punched in the Game Commission's number again. Still busy. We stood around. The fawn had bled through Marj's shirt onto her lap and blood had spotted the car seat. I didn't care. I called a third time. Busy. Furious now that a large agency didn't have enough telephone lines for someone to get through in an emergency and incensed in the first place over an incomprehensible rule that allows an animal to suffer because of an arbitrary distinction between wildness and domesticity, I called our vet back and begged him to put the baby deer out of its misery and us out of ours. Reluctantly, he agreed. We raced into town, the fawn quiet in Marj's lap, lulled by the motion of the car.

Phil and I waited outside the vet's treatment room, our eyes on his back as he fiddled with something I wasn't sure he'd heard us enter but, shortly, he turned, syringe in hand, and led us out to the parking lot. We opened the passenger door and Marj swiveled in her seat so the vet could reach the deer's good foreleg. He found a vein, and as the fluid entered it, the baby deer's head slowly lolled over on its side. Done—swiftly and painlessly. I wept at the perfection of such an easy dying. The vet waved away our offered payment.

We placed the fawn's body in a plastic bag (being sure, at my insistence, not to cover its head—you know, smother it), and when we got home, laid it on the porch. Marj went upstairs to bathe her arms, which had developed red welts from an allergic reaction to the deer, while I threw our clothes into the laundry with hot water and bleach, thoroughly washed my hands, and prepared our lunch.

When Henderson came home that afternoon, he and Phil went up into the woods and dug a deep grave on a knoll. When they came down, I hoisted up the bag and was surprised at how much heavier the fawn seemed, dead. Phil carried it up the hill. Marj lined the hole with her blood-soaked outer shirt. We placed the baby deer, minus plastic bag, on top, and H and Phil shoveled in the dirt.

Marj, an animal rights activist, said that when she got home she would see if she could fight this law that prevents a veterinarian from treating or putting down a wild animal. Both she and I wrote our vet, effusively thanking him for his compassionate service and omitting any possibly incriminating specifics. Last week, when I took our dogs there for shots, I noticed that our two letters were prominently displayed on the bulletin board next to the front door.

Even without such incidents, it takes me a week to recover from a guest weekend and the days of preparation that precede it. You'd have to look closely at me to see that the manic energy that flattens anyone in my path who is just standing around, not doing his share (Henderson), is really a frenzy of self-castigation. Every hole in my personality must be stoppered before the guests arrive; every flaw in the house hunted down, exposed to light, repaired; every rough edge smoothed—you get the picture. If the tone of this essay does not lead you to conclude that I myself am big-eyed with fear before the arrival of guests, it only testifies to my acting ability, even on paper.

The relative seclusion we've enjoyed for so many years makes entertaining unexpectedly difficult. Preparing gourmet meals, keeping up my end of a nonstop conversation, and imagining myself through the eyes of strangers is emotionally exhausting. What is especially nerve-wracking about having guests is that I'm jerked into looking at myself and our home from the outside, through hard, critical eyes— not the guests', in all probability, but my own.

Flaws that don't bother me in the least when guests are not expected—cobwebs, dog hairs, wood stove soot—point accusing fingers at me the minute I've booked a weekend. I clean cupboards and drawers that will never be opened while guests are here. I can't help myself.

Eighteen years after we began renovating it, the house is still not quite finished—we have only plywood floors in the living room, mostly covered with large oval braided rugs in forest green and burgundy, but plywood underneath. Now there's a new grease stain on the floor by Henderson's chair. We came by the *old* foot-wide blotches honestly—we used to park our chainsaws indoors for the winter so their fluids would be liquid enough to start up. The fluids leaked. I'm used to the old blotches, but this new one bothers me as if I, too, had sprung a leak when I wasn't looking.

It occurs to me that what I've been trying to do at the Gray Ghost these last 18 years is set a scene where punishing migraines and chronic self-criticism flatten me less often, where, in fact, I might begin to feel as taken care of as I try to make our guests feel. But what I've most clearly succeeded in doing, at least in the case of the Gray Ghost Guesthouse, is merely set the scene by setting the table. In the case of the Heartland Foods health food business, we had to build the stage. And in order to make our home at Gray Ghost Farm in the first place, we had to construct the entire theater!

On with the show.

AT HOME

WRITING ON MOWING

It is as if life is forever trying to keep itself exquisitely
balanced on the edge between chaos and order, always about to
fall into the imprisoning forces of an overly ordered world on one side
and the seductive calls of complete chaos on the other.

David Whyte, *The Heart Aroused*

My twin sisters, six years older than I, hit their teens and
sprouted up. They grew tall—not only taller than I, of
course, but considerably taller than other girls their own age. Mother
used to call them the big girls and a bit ruefully referred to me, of
normal height, as the runt. Neither of these labels did us any favors.
In fact, although my sisters are now 63 years old and I am 57, I still
believe that when I really grow up I'll finally be tall, too.

My sisters talked a lot faster and louder than I did then. At dinner,
we sat around a rectangular dining room table in a configuration that
turned out not to be helpful in keeping me off an analyst's couch in

later years: My tall mother and my tall father sat at opposite ends, and my two tall, fast-talking, and rivetingly animated sisters sat together on one long side opposite little, dumbfounded, awestruck me all alone in the middle of the other side. When one sister drew a breath or took a mouthful, the other continued to regale our parents with news of their day's events.

This is a shorthand explanation of how come deep down I'm still scared I'm little and of no account. Invisible, even. Why else would I have grown up to be so intense, opinionated, irreverent? I can't for a minute relax my vigilance when it comes to making sure I'm noticed.

Therefore, I avoid "being" activities like meditation, where the object is to become one with something greater than oneself—the universe, God—and favor instead doing things where I can make an impact, see myself reflected. In the ten years I lived in Philadelphia, I bought and renovated seven houses, and then moved to the country and totally restored an abandoned farmhouse with my husband. One long exhale later, we added a small country health food store. Last August, we built a big barn for our goats.

So when it comes to a choice between sitting down at the computer and writing or doing something where I can impose myself on my environment—like, say, running out and mowing the lawn—you guessed it. Whereas my best writing self might not be available that day, I can never fail at mowing. My appetite for mowing is directly proportional to my degree of anxiety while waiting for green thoughts at the computer.

I keep a small stable of walk-behind gas-powered lawn mowers—three mowing machines for a two-acre lawn. Now, two acres is a lot of lawn—the area around the house up to where the woods begin alone takes three hours to level—but by no means is two acres vast enough to warrant owning three mowers.

It's not that I'm particularly proud of the fleet itself. In fact, I'm so indifferent to the machines that I use them too hard and sympathize too little when they're exhausted, which is the reason I have three in the first place—one is always in the shop. And for a couple of weeks there last June—the frantic growing and therefore mowing season, the month when the dandelions merely duck when they see me and my mower coming and spring right back up after we've passed over—both Lawnboys were in the shop. I had to buy another one. Besides, I'd always wanted a Troybilt.

I'm eager to discuss mowing, and I raise the subject at the least provocation. I eye the postman's tan appreciatively and inquire with a wink, "Mowing?" "Golf," he corrects me. I turn to go in with a sniff. But the UPS driver's tan I know is from mowing; it's darker on Mondays because he cuts his three acres over the weekend, using a ride-on. We've debated the advantages of cutting around in diminishing squares, or back and forth parallel to the first cut line. Nowadays, I don't dare do squares. My mowers have begun to rattle and ting and I know they're dreaming of time off in the shop, so back and forth I go along the same cut line. Then, if they quit before I'm finished, there won't be a square right in the middle of the lawn that my eye will obsessively cut over and over from my bed where I gaze out through the balcony doors, drinking my morning coffee.

It has taken me some time to understand my mania for mowing. In fact, most of the time when I'm mowing, I'm also writing this essay in my head, trying to figure out why I love it so much. I've wondered if there might be some hidden meaning in the word *mow* itself.

Nope, although just saying the word *mowing* softens me. Mowing. It's as close to flowing as I get. Then maybe the significance is in the word spelled backward: *wom*. A friend suggested that WOM is an acronym for Woman Obsessed with Mowing.

But I'm not really so obsessive about it. I never mow until the grass is about three inches high. There's certainly no pleasure in mowing until I can see progress. The whole point, after all, is the visual pleasure of closely cropped lawn rolling up to wild hayfield and forest—from short to high, groomed to wild.

Sitting quietly next to my grass-green mower at the top of the hill, smelling the freshly mown cuttings, I gaze back over the expanse at the slanting sunlight bumping and stretching over the hummocks and hillocks that shape my tiny arc of globe. Resting my eyes on this unobstructed view of broad lawn helps me breathe deeply. It's evening. My work is obviously done. There is nothing more I can be expected to do tonight.

My appetite for ordering my world is large indeed, sometimes excessive; I'll start out intending to mow only one section of lawn before going in, but when I'm nearly finished, I can't keep myself from going right over and chopping off a section of high grass along the edge. Now that, too, becomes part of the lawn, and forever after needs mowing.

Normally I hate tasks that seem endless, where progress is difficult to measure, like gathering kindling or piling brush or keeping a journal, like living life itself, which is accomplished by small, steady movements, persistent accretion, instead of great grand sweeps of effort. But mowing, that relentless staking of my claim, claiming more and more wilderness each year and thumbing my nose at Nature—

now that's the dumb grunt labor for me. In fact, it's the only monotonous labor I'd almost kill to do—kill mowers, at least; almost kill myself, if heat-induced migraines could kill. Once I almost slit my throat, mowing.

I saw the piece of wire there in the grass. Did I think it would shred into a thousand pieces like the small branches I grind up? Didn't I realize the tiny shards might end up in a goat's stomach? I didn't stop for the second it would have taken to bend down and pocket it. I mowed right over it. Up it shot instantly and sliced a two-inch-long bright red streak in my shoulder. Could have been my jugular, my cheek, my eyeball. Instead of several seconds out of my mowing day, I spent two hours in the emergency room of the local hospital being stitched.

Deep down I know that if I had all the time in the world, instead of sitting at my keyboard where thoughts erupt willy-nilly in tangles like new growth—or worse, like weeds, or worse yet, erupt not at all—I'd follow my mowers over the entire 20 acres of hayfield (winter hay for the goats be damned!), and then I'd go in and cut out all the dead wood in the 50 acres of forest and turn the whole thing into a tidy park. But habitat for the little forest creatures is safe. I'll surely die exerting my will on the areas I've already selected.

Besides, I can avoid writing only so long, although getting to my desk is often a terrible struggle. Good writing requires a harmonious interplay between allowing and controlling and as such represents my central dilemma of finding that "exquisite balance" between doing and being. Yet when I'm writing, I get to live life twice, once in the yard and again at the computer. I find out what I think, hear my voice, and see, quite concretely, that someone who is invisible and of no account could not have written down those observations that spare nobody, including herself. Why, then, I must exist. So I am drawn, as if it were my soul's prime mandate, to make sense of my days and by doing so, practice tender patience with that little girl at the dining room table who has a strong voice now.

Mowing and writing may not be opposites after all. Mowing might be a kind of meditation during which I end up unwittingly blending with something larger than myself. Mowing appears to slow time because it forces me to make and complete each swipe before going on to the next, trusting that the mown swaths will add up. Dare I say it? Trusting the process.

The trick is to satisfy my need to be doing: keep the arms and legs moving, engage in a project with a beginning, middle, and end, with tangible, visually pleasing results, and cross something off the list at the end of it. While my arms and legs are busy fulfilling my compulsion to accomplish something, my unconscious is sometimes writing the next essay—a blessing in double productivity!

Perhaps I can sneak past my writer's block if I approach writing like mowing. I'll sit at the computer for two to three hours, write small pieces with beginnings, middles, and ends, explore one specific subject until I've smoothed its bumps—writing from the top down, imposing order as I go.

Or maybe writing can't be done this way. Maybe the only way to generate ideas is to wait at my humming computer, staring at its blinking yellow cursor, emptyheaded, feet planted, arms dangling, stripped of the comforts of my compulsions, right in the swirling midst of anxiety, allowing my mind to wander, suffering the prospect of disappearing into useless thoughts, allowing the grass to grow outside my window, and hoping for shoots of creativity to inch up inside my brain.

God forbid my own motor conks out before I've dared dip into the chaos of my unconscious in the hope of emerging with something of value, something more lasting than a mown lawn—one fine essay, perhaps, that would prove that I am sitting at this table and that I have a voice.

THE END

The most that any one of us can seem to do is to
fashion something—an object or ourselves—
and drop it into the confusion, make an offering of it,
so to speak, to the life force.

Ernest Becker, *The Denial of Death*

We're down to five goats, two dogs, and four cats, now, but until early this year our farmstead supported a full complement of pets and livestock—24 animals in all, if you counted the nine hens. The newest additions to the menagerie were a pair of husky/hound dog puppies, given to us by our neighbor Sal two summers ago.

"How'd you like to step back in time ten years?" Sal had called out the window of his car as he drove up to where my husband, Henderson, and I were stacking wood. We looked at him quizzically and walked over to the car. The puppies were entwined in a big box on his back seat. I lifted first one and then the other, and melted.

Same thing ten years ago: big box on back seat, me goo-goo eyed over the two German Shepherd puppies therein, whom I named Fanny and Teddy. Toby, our Labrador retriever who has since died, was elderly, but we didn't need three dogs then, and we certainly didn't need four dogs now. But I'm a sucker for a puppy face. Caramel-colored Dalton, with his blue "watch" eye, and his sister, timorous gray Waverly, came on board.

With their addition, the accumulation of animals at Gray Ghost Farm ended and the long attrition phase began. It began rather suddenly, it turned out, when, last spring, Dalton discovered he could squeeze under the fence that surrounds the dog yard. In a burst of adolescent exuberance, he ate his way through the entire brood of hens. Each day for a week I found newly mangled bodies scattered about the upper yard and into the woods, their stomachs rent. I could peer into their bellies and see already-formed eggs, shells and all.

Each time I found a dead chicken, I walloped Dalton, but because I never caught him in the act of murder, he accepted this punishment with some bewilderment. A local farmer said to tie a dead chicken to his neck. I did. Dalton flattened himself on the ground and accepted this fate with what seemed like genuine remorse. Then he liberated himself by biting through the baling twine. He wagged his tail and pranced about, eager to regain my approval.

It was difficult to stay angry at so otherwise simple and guileless a dog, but in order to kiss a face that had killed chickens, I had to crank myself into a philosophic attitude by ranking the two species by preference. Which did I feel greater kinship with—*canis* or *Gallus*

gallus? All the chickens were dead by this time, so the point was moot. Besides, I am a product of the nurture (versus nature) school of psychology (if beating a dog can be construed as nurture), as it supports my illusion that I control things. Even the canine temperament is not beyond my influence. I believed Dalton would outgrow the habit. It never occurred to me that the dogs would take on larger game.

In March, as we were loading the car for a weekend out of town, Dalton and Waverly slipped out under their fence again—a fence we had patched repeatedly, you should know—and streaked off toward the woods. I called them back sternly. I called them again, using my most imperative tone, but they merely paused, looked back, consulted each other, and agreed, "Nah, she's not serious." Dalton was the ringleader. I could almost hear him call back over his shoulder to Waverly, "Psst, Wave, quick. Follow me."

We knew they'd return home eventually. All we were worried about, at that point, was that harm might come to them in our absence. We were gone only overnight, and when we turned into the driveway the next evening, they crawled out from under the porch, wagging and wiggling and twining themselves around our legs, and we greeted them with relief. Mature Teddy and Fanny were wiggling and wagging from behind the fence.

The next morning, I looked out an upstairs window into the goat yard. Capricorn, our 12-year-old buck, was lying on his side motionless on the cold ground. His head lay in a small rivulet that had been released by the spring thaw. "Sleeping," I hoped for a fleeting moment. Hardly. A goat would not rest his head in water. Capricorn had been losing weight for months and was hobbled by arthritis in his back legs, but he enjoyed my daily brushing and, aside from his obvious discomfort when walking, still seemed interested in living. I did not think it was time for the vet. As I approached his body, I saw tufts of hair and hide scattered on the ground around him. His groin, the fastest way to his entrails, had been chewed. I don't think it was the chewing itself that killed him—the skin was abraded but not ripped open. I think the cause of death was a heart attack brought on by the terror of being selected, taunted, chased, and inevitably run down; a heart attack because he was an old goat, crippled and in failing health; a heart attack because he was forced, in those last moments, to comprehend the inevitability of the hoofprints on the wall.

But even after this, I didn't turn against the dogs. "Capricorn would have died soon anyway," I told Henderson. "Dalton and Waverly merely culled the herd. It's in the nature of a hound dog to hound and dog a weaker animal." The puppies wiggled and waggled and licked my hands and face, and again I discounted their dark aspect.

A few months later, though, they struck again. They'd gotten loose, but this time we were home, pruning some pine trees below the house. Suddenly, we heard loud, anguished cries that we recognized immediately as the blatting of a terrified goat. Our closest neighbor, whose house is several football fields down the hill, heard it too. He jumped on his four-wheeler and raced up the road to help. The dogs had cornered GG in the orchard, one on each side of her, barking. She had stumbled, trying to face both attackers at once, and fallen. She was struggling to rise, and she was bellowing. It's not a sound you can easily forget, and it's not a sound you want to hear on your farm—the sound of one of your beloved goats being bullied by your sweet, now vicious, puppies. It did not take a full minute this time to know which species I favored.

Dalton went to the pound the next day. He was a handsome dog, even-tempered and obedient except for this character flaw. It grieved me to abandon him to a small, cold cage. I called the SPCA later that week to see if he'd been adopted. He hadn't, yet. I didn't call back.

I spared Waverly because she was an ingratiating omega to the older, alpha dogs, Teddy and Fanny. I figured that she had merely succumbed to pack mentality. If separated, probably neither of the dogs would have attacked alone, or the one more likely to would have been rough-and-tumble Dalton, not my sweet, shy Waverly.

It's been a hard year. The events, in chronological order, are these: In November, Henderson's uncle died. When relatives phoned Henderson's father to tell him that his brother was dead, they got no answer. The phone rang and rang and rang. Finally, they drove out to the house and banged on his door. Still no answer. One of the men climbed in through a window and found Alexander dead on the living room floor from a heart attack. The coroner said the brothers had died on the same day.

In January, Henderson was driving to work one morning when the truck slid on a patch of ice, sailed off an embankment into a farmer's pasture, and turned over twice, heels over head, before coming to a stop right side up. Henderson crawled out the driver's window, shaken but unharmed. The truck was totaled.

In February, my 61-year-old sister Julie, twin to our other sister, Penny, was diagnosed with ALS, the wasting disease Lou Gehrig died from. She first noticed something wrong last October, when she found she needed to reach around with her left hand to help her right hand turn the key in the car's ignition switch. Now, a year later, her right arm flops at her side—she can't wash her left armpit, can't dress herself, can't wipe herself. With her left hand she can still spoon food into her mouth, but she can't fold laundry, pare vegetables, wash dishes, carry a cup of coffee or a glass of wine across the room. Her legs are going, too. There is not a chair in her house she can get up from without her husband's assistance. She's had to retire from a long acting career at Theater Three on Long Island, where she played leads and supporting roles since graduating from the American Academy of Dramatic Arts in the same class as Robert Redford. She can't turn the pages of a script.

The usual course of this disease, which has no known treatment and no remissions, is progressive muscle weakening leading to death in two to five years, making it unlikely that Julie will reach 66, the age at which our mother died of cancer. In all probability, Julie will predecease our 90-year-old father, whose heart, despite a stroke six years ago, steadily sloshes blood to all the necessary organs without sign of fatigue. Paralyzed on his left side and wheelchair-bound in a nursing home, Daddy keeps eating the three servings of unidentifiable mash they put in front of him each day, vowing to live to 100. He survived Mother's death by 22 years and, just recently, the death of her sister, to whom he was married for those same 22 years. His daughters call him every day and marvel that he still finds life worth living. We think we'd die from the boredom alone, but perhaps the 90-year-old brain doesn't crave stimulation as ours do.

I was surprised when Mother died, then angry at myself for being surprised, for being so naive at age 33 to think that all the deaths I'd heard about on the news and read about had nothing to do with me. How could a piece of me still think my loved ones and I would get out alive?

Now that I've let death in, now that the fragile skin of death-denial is terminally rent, everything else I hear or read tears the membrane further until death is everywhere. My college roommate's son died this year. He was 27. He was boating on the lake with friends when he was stung by a bee. He was dead before they reached the shore.

Now, under every moment lurks the big dark thing. Does the arthritis in my big toe foreshadow something? How about the pain in my left elbow? All I can think to do in the face of nothing to do about my sister's diagnosis is to slowly or quickly kill myself—by overeating, overdrinking, and taking up smoking again after 14 years.

But I know that spring is just as true as death. In a few months I'll be mowing the lawns and weeding the gardens, performing the ultimate betrayal—exercising my muscles as Julie's are atrophying, just as if I planned to continue using them, just as if I were choosing life, even as Julie is dying.

In April, 12-year-old Teddy stopped eating. The vet drew blood, diagnosed him with extensive liver damage, and didn't hold out much hope for the antibiotics he sent us home with. Teddy, thin and very sweet, slept most of his final days. His back legs wobbled when he stood up, and his body swayed. Shortly, his legs would buckle beneath him. He was barely able to stand long enough to explode with diarrhea, usually in the yard, but sometimes in the kitchen, where we surrounded him with newspapers. All day Sunday and Monday I read beside him while he lay on his side, occasionally lifting his head with difficulty, looking at me with doleful, uncomprehending eyes.

Teddy was a needy dog. On walks, when he was a puppy, he'd whine to be carried after a half-mile. Later, when he was a big dog, how often I had to urge him to go "Out!" which really meant, "Dammit, Teddy, go *away*! Unglue yourself from my side!" Wanting to be close to me, but unsure how to comply with my "Out!" order and still be near, he'd circle around and walk directly behind me, so close he'd step on my heels, causing more loud outbursts from me, which further shamed him and further increased his need for approval and forgiveness.

On walks, Teddy took his shepherding duties to heart, needing to bump us with his nose every few minutes to be sure we were coming along. He'd run ahead, think better of it, circle back, and bang his nose into our legs, leaving a skid mark of drool. He'd dash off again, turn back, and repeat the ritual.

Men had to be careful of their crotches, which, just at the height of Teddy's head, often got punched by Teddy's needle nose. He'd gather steam running toward them and then not be able to stop before sliding his snout several inches into the wedge of light between their legs.

In his older, mellower years, as I, too, had mellowed, his habits charmed me. Now, while the puppies and Fanny tore off in all directions, Teddy walked by my side as sedately as if we'd been successful in training him to heel, which we hadn't been. I would pat his head and call him my "good stick-by-me-boy."

Teddy was a nosy dog and a *noisy* one. Dropping down beside my reading chair, the collapse of body against floor forced air across his vocal cords, causing him to express a long, sonorous groan of satisfaction. When I'd put on my boots for our w-a-l-k (I had to spell it) he'd prance around, yawning compulsively and emitting a range of high squeaks that sounded like a series of questions. Telling him to be quiet was futile. He'd try, but the squeaks, the *eeks*, came out anyway, followed by a hangdog droop around the eyes. He knew he was annoying but couldn't help himself. This was a dog people loved to be exasperated by. I remember saying that only a mother could put up with the eeks, and sometimes, even she....

In his final days, there were no eeks left. When he could no longer stand and everything had shut down—nothing in, nothing out—we put him on a quilt in the back of the Subaru and drove him to the vet. Henderson told the receptionist we were in the parking lot while I waited on the tailgate beside Teddy. Tailgate euthanasia means less hoisting and schlepping of the ailing animal. It means not having to walk in through a crowded waiting room with a live dog and then walk out, a few minutes later, with a dead one.

After a time, the vet came out with the equipment. The previous week, Teddy had bolted when the same vet inserted a needle to draw his blood, and we'd had to hold tight to keep him from squirming off the table. One week later, he didn't even raise his head as the catheter entered his ulnar vein.

The vet asked me if I would like to inject the serum. Yes, yes, I would, I said. Two syringes were to be emptied into the catheter. The first, a tranquilizer, slowed Teddy's breathing perceptibly.

Then, weeping steadily, I kissed the side of Teddy's long nose and told him how much we had really loved him. I slowly pushed in the plunger of the second syringe, which was filled with a cheery, Pepto-Bismol-pink serum. He was gone instantly. We brought him home and placed him in the deep grave Henderson had dug on the hill above the house. As the sun set, we filled in the hole and drank to Teddy, Capricorn, and our first dog, Toby.

I have to face a fact that had somehow escaped me until this year: With 24 animals under our care, all 24 will die on our watch. Either that or we will die, and who knows what will happen to the animals. Or, some of them will die under our care and then we'll die, and then, eventually, the rest of the animals will die. In any case, as much as there has been lots of life on our farm, from now on there will be lots of dying.

Frankly, I prefer death to come to those I love from the tip of a needle, a toxin-filled needle that, ideally, I administer myself. So far, no vet has agreed to slip me a few prefilled syringes for home use. Buthanesia (a barbiturate given in overdose amount) is a controlled substance for good reason. If I ever get my hands on a vial, I'll put down my husband, when his time comes, and if my time comes before his, I'll put myself down. I'm going to figure out a way to do it, anyway. Watch me.

September 15: GG—the goat we named Gray Goat, a takeoff on the name we call our farmhouse, the Gray Ghost—can't stand up. It has nothing to do with the dog attack. For weeks, she's not been eating her grain. She's been losing weight, and now her belly is bloated. She has collapsed on her side in the barn doorway. I tried lifting her front end, but her back legs don't work, and she's too heavy for me to lift both ends at once with my arms around her middle, slinglike. When Henderson gets home, we'll move her into a corner of the barn so the other goats don't tread on her. For now, I take a lawn chair and a book and sit beside her. I wrap my vest and wind-breaker more tightly around me as I stroke her bony head and neck. The autumn breeze is brisk, and when the swift white clouds scuttle across the sun, the temperature drops noticeably. I zip up my jacket and keep on stroking.

Although GG is not one of my very favorite goats, she has an agreeable, if bland, personality. She's a follower—well, somebody has to constitute the herd. She's prone to bloat each spring after eating the bright green, protein-rich shoots of early grass, and to relieve her, we stick a fat syringe in the side of her mouth and squirt mineral oil down her gullet. I massage her belly, the way Henderson and I do for each other, encouraging the gas bubbles around, down, and out.

September 16: Yesterday, when Henderson got home, we made a temporary sick bay by enclosing one corner of the barn with upended pallets. GG can't rise even to evacuate, so after a day of her lying in her own urine we must drag her out, sponge her off with warm water, and prepare another corner, Cloroxing the concrete floor in the first. Her urine is foul-smelling and caustic, probably the result of ketosis, a byproduct of starvation. We roll GG onto a large piece of cardboard to use as a sled. Her belly, taut as a tick's, doesn't collapse to the down side, as it normally would, but stays mountained up. Her eyes bulge and roll back into their sockets, showing mostly white; her mouth drops open, exposing her bottom teeth; her tongue lolls out. I think she is going to die here and now. The pain of being moved must have taken her breath away, for she doesn't utter a sound. I quickly douse her belly with warm water and roll her back. We haul her into the new corner so she can dry on a thick blanket of hay. GG's rumen must be filled with tiny gas bubbles that she can't belch up, and spasmodic dry retching has failed to bring up her cud. Her digestive system is kaput. To Henderson I say, "Enough."

September 17: The vet has come and gone. He brought his pistol, he told me, in case I preferred that method. He told me that if we went with the poison, we'd have to bury GG at least three feet down. Buthanesia is so virulent and long-lasting that it could kill any wildlife—or the dogs—if they dug her up and ate her.

Until now, I've enjoyed the idea that all the animals will be buried up on Hoof Hill, but it's a romantic notion and something of an indulgence. Because I don't have the strength in my arms and shoulders to dig a deep grave in our rocky soil, Henderson would have to do it, and it's not a considerate chore to give a man when he comes off an eight-hour shift of heavy lifting down at the recycling plant. So, because the grave could be shallower, I considered the pistol method.

"You'd put the gun right next to her temple?"

"No," he said, "into her eyeball."

"Oh," said I. "Let's go with the poison and you can take her body and cremate it."

My good friend Dan Vickers, now in his sixties, is an addiction counselor who gained his credentials 40 years ago as a heroin addict. At one rehab facility back then, he complained to his therapist of deep depression with suicidal thoughts. His therapist asked him how serious he was about committing suicide. Dan answered, "Dead serious."

"Okay," said his therapist. "Here's how you do it. You get a gun and you put the barrel of it right here, into your eyeball, like this. Then you pull the trigger."

Dan has been recovered ever since.

I'm not saying that one ghoulish instruction from a guy with a sense of humor did it, but you gotta admit that picturing the results of this method does blow a rather large hole in the idea of suicide as a dramatic statement.

The vet and I enter the barn. Belinda, Ivy, Rosemary, Daisy, and Sweet William come to greet us. In her pen, GG raises her head, her ears twitching forward with the curiosity so characteristic of goats.

I went to a livestock auction once. When the gate between the holding pens and the bidding arena was opened, the first group, the sheep, huddled in a logjam in the doorway and had to be prodded forward. But when it was time for the goats to be auctioned, each one trotted forth smartly into the arena, curiosity and perhaps an inclination to trust humans overriding caution.

I kneel down beside GG in the hay and cradle her head in my arms, gently pulling it up and toward me so that the vet has a clear shot at her jugular. I press my cheek against her nose and softly croon good-bye. In the seconds it takes to empty the syringe, her head slumps in my arms. The membrane separating life from death is so very, very thin. There are final spasms and exhalations, but the vet assures me her brain is dead. If you can put your finger right on the eyeball, he says, and the animal doesn't blink or pull away, she's dead. The other goats are milling around, munching hay, untroubled.

The vet delivers a cursory post-mortem diagnosis: caprine arthritis encephalitis—goat AIDS. Joint swelling and pain, loss of appetite, and wasting are symptoms. As we're no longer selling their milk or breeding the goats, we'll be their rest home—they're all over ten years old. Knowing that their ends will likely be as swift and painless as GG's, we can enjoy their remaining years without a cloud of worry over their final days. I dearly wish we could say that with certainty about our human loved ones.

I like to think of GG meeting up with Capricorn at that great grain bin in the sky, as Henderson calls it.

September 18: So we're down to five goats, and, from the looks of it, going down fast. The very next day after the vet left, Ivy began favoring her left leg. I checked to make sure there wasn't a stone between her toes. There wasn't, but she's been limping steadily. And Sweet William, Capricorn's erstwhile rival, spends too much time on his bent front knees, as if in prayer. His legs must be arthritic and, given his great hulk, standing must be painful. It's as though once recognized and named, this virus has gained more than a toehold.

I'm sorry if Ivy should go next—before, say, Daisy. Daisy has a vanilla personality stippled with black moments of sheer meanness toward the other goats and toward Ivy in particular. She's nice enough to me—I have a photo of Daisy and me stretching our noses toward each other, practically kissing, that was taken by my sister Julie when she visited a few years ago. Daisy has the most perfect breasts, a full, pendulous udder with firm, symmetrical teats that are squeezably, milkably soft, delightful to handle. And Daisy is Henderson's favorite goat, perhaps because she's not my favorite. He had to stake his claim somewhere. But if she and Sweet William were to die, I'd still have my three favorite goats: Ivy, Rosemary, and Belinda.

Typically, the goats gather around me when I come through the gate, but if I make a sudden move to stroke their noses, they jerk their heads away, indicating that they're not like dogs, slavishly groveling to be petted. They come to me and, gently, I can go to them, but sudden moves and great demonstrations of affection are politely discouraged. This is true for all the goats except Ivy.

Here's a video of my relationship with Ivy: I am striding across the hayfield, home from my morning walk with the dogs. The goats are browsing in the orchard, under the apple trees. As I move toward them, they look up and acknowledge me with soft guttural hums. Then, one goat separates herself from the herd and begins trotting toward me across the field. It is Miss Ivy. The morning light diffuses, the image blurs, violins commence a tremolo. We are that romantic couple in the commercial of a man and a maiden approaching each other in slo-mo from opposite sides of the screen through the lilies of the field. It is Ivy and I, running toward each other—at any minute, I think, she'll grow alarmed as my size increases and will veer off—but she keeps trotting toward me, her flanks bouncing like saddlebags. I fall to my knees, spread wide my arms, and throw them around her neck as she runs into them. She stands there, panting, while I stroke her and hug her and kiss her in the hollow between her eyeball socket and her ear (my favorite place because, being out of the way, it's less likely to be dusty). I kiss her cheeks and she whispers in my ear that she could stand like this forever.

Rosemary, the goat I—I nursed, I almost wrote—the goat I bottle-fed (close enough)—Rosie's been known to get up on her hind legs and point the top of her head (where her horns used to be) at you, which is not a friendly thing to do. She did it once to guests who were housesitting and once to Henderson. She's never done it to me. I can't blame Henderson for cooling toward her after this, though I suspect he was never going to love her because she was "my" goat from the start. I think Rosemary still considers me her mother. She plunks herself down beside my lawn chair and lets herself be gently petted, but I have to tame my ebullience with Rosie; I can't lovingly manhandle her the way I can Ivy. But of all of the goats, Rosie's still seated at my side when the others have moseyed on to lusher grass. While it's not the high romance I have with Ivy, ours is a natural blood bond. Or we're an old married couple, so grounded in love that we don't have to display it by running through the fields.

The herd queen, our first goat, is Belinda. Each morning, Belinda sets out from the barn on a foraging trip up the hill, leading her family single-file into the meadow for browsing, her alpine nose thrust forward, her lean, strong body graceful and deliberate. She leads with purpose, as if she knows exactly where the grass will be most nutritious on that particular day. After an hour or so, she lifts her head and, with equal certitude, leads them back to the barn to digest in the shade. It's easy to imagine Belinda as a grand dame, a lady. Never silly or frivolous, never begging for attention, she stands soberly beside my chair allowing her nose to be petted. If I stop, though, she moves closer and hangs her head into the *V* of my open book until I'm reading Belinda.

I've noticed a mean streak in Belinda that I tend to forget when extolling her noble attributes. She has it in for Ivy, her one remaining daughter. She seems to look for opportunities to ram Ivy in the side, and Ivy, defenseless and perhaps not very bright (shhh...), is invariably caught completely by surprise. I scold Belinda and swat at her, but she smartly ducks away. I vow to carry a fly swatter with me to extend my reach, but I don't. I'm trying to allow some aspects of nature to take their course. Besides, do I really want Ivy's welfare to depend on my intercession? I'd have to be in the barn 24/7.

Including this prickly characteristic in the mix that is Belinda gives me a different take on her queendom. Perhaps she's not even aware that the herd's following her. Perhaps, in fact, she doesn't give a damn. She's not "leading her family"; no maternal instinct here, just total concentration on her own gastric needs. She's taking herself up the hill to greener pastures. If the others follow, so be it.

This makes me wonder if, over the years, I myself have become like Belinda, if my fierce independence isn't more a certain ruthlessness. I've noticed in the last few years that I lack generosity, lack the interest I had in saving mankind. My days could be characterized by a narrowing of focus, and in that way I am like Belinda.

Each morning I awaken impelled by a feeling of urgency, a powerful sense that time is running out. I don't waste it. I march through life as though there were a deadly seriousness at the heart of it, as if it really mattered that I milk some satisfaction from each day. It does matter. It really is time-limited, life.

The ruthlessness, if that's what it is, conceals what I've always known made up my gelatinous essence—wobbly self-doubt. Yet, even about my own neurosis, I lack generosity. I can't be bothered trying to recreate dark incidents that would explain a lifelong commitment to self-criticism. Even if I could, my allotment of insecurity would probably turn out to be no greater than yours. My parents were happily married for 41 years. I grew up in material comfort with intelligent people who deliberated their decisions regarding our upbringing and provided us with consistency and stability.

Daddy was charming, courtly, agreeable, funny, Harvard-educated.

Mother had a bristly personality, but I alone of the three daughters reacted poorly to it. I, alone, felt undermined by her judgments. Maybe she judged only me. Maybe she was a different person by the time I was born. Raising twins for six years could change a person, knock some of the patience out of her, sharpen her personality. Who knows? All I know is that by the time I was on my third or fourth psychiatrist, I was able to articulate my deep conviction that I had done something dreadful as a child. Killed another child. I've gone through life believing, as I know many people do on some level, that if "they" really knew the truth about me, I'd be in for the full-scale condemnation I surely deserve.

After reading hundreds of memoirs, my complaining about Mother's domineering disposition and her subtle censure sounds like whining. She had a personality, is all. I reacted badly to it. If I developed corrosive self-doubt, well, I had to acquire some sort of personality as I grew up, and this is the one that evolved out of the particular alchemy of me in that family.

Besides, how could the message that it is unwise to show vulnerability have been grooved so deeply and as early as infancy? And has all the growing up I've done since been merely to calcify scar tissue over an original wound? Could it be that I haven't transformed any of it into wisdom but merely buried it in layers of personality? Are we all permanently skewed by parental misdeeds in the first few years of life, living out the rest of our days as our branch was first bent? The inexorableness of this, not to mention the inevitability that my own mistakes as a parent have indelibly scarred my daughter, is overwhelming. It's enough to make me think about putting a pistol to my eyeball.

How is it I can speak so easily about killing myself when, on a bright fall day like today, I am so very pleased to be alive? Because if I were to kill myself it would be on a rainy day, not on a day like today.

Then I realize that if I were dying, I'd be dying on the glorious days, too.

Every death takes a bite out of you until, by the time you're old, you're emotional Swiss cheese. What I'll do when all the goats have died, I don't know. It saddens me to picture the barn empty. Then I consider the hole Julie's death will leave in the lives of her husband, her sisters, her grown sons, and her little granddaughter, and my mind skitters away from the thought as if touched by fire. It is possible to prepare for and describe the death of a goat. It is nearly impossible to contain all the elements of a sororal relationship, let alone imagine its disappearance.

Julie and I corresponded intermittently during the years when we were raising our children. Then, when I moved to Philadelphia 20 years ago, she wrote and began to visit me regularly. I'd meet her train at the 30th Street station, where she'd wait for me under a huge, bronze statue of a winged man—the Angel of Death, we decided he was. When Henderson and I moved to this farm, Julie visited even more often, and throughout the last two years when I was suffering through graduate school, she assumed the copyediting of my thesis manuscript. The gift of her time and attention was the best mothering.

Death is the dirtiest trick in the book, and frankly, it gives me pause about life. It makes me loath to play the living game if these are the rules. Of course, most of the time you wake up and find that you haven't died, and that nobody you know has died, which lulls you into the false impression that it's an ordered universe and that you're in control of your life to some measure. And that is not entirely *un*true. You do postpone your death by taking care, fastening your seat belt, looking both ways before crossing, not running with scissors, etc.

But to be sure the end of my life is under my control, a part of me considers killing myself now.

So here's a video of my relationship with death: I am running just a few steps ahead of death with a knife in my hands, ready to plunge it into my heart the moment death signals me. I turn and taunt the cloaked shape behind me. "Aha!" I grin. "You thought *you'd* get me. Watch this. Watch this. I'll get *myself*!" (My life's metaphor—say all the bad things I can think of about myself before anyone else can, inoculating myself against censure. Immunity, after all, is a kind of control.)

So there I am, and death is marching toward me. I'm holding the knife high over my head, ready to thrust it into my abdomen. Death marches on, inexorably. Now death *seems* to be looking at me, but really he's looking at the person just over my left shoulder, and there I am grinning madly, the knife trembling in my hands. Death picks up speed, now, and dashes toward me, and just before he veers off to tap the person on my left, I plunge the knife into my belly with triumph. As he scurries past, he gives me a look that says, "Jeez. What a loony!"

In *Intoxicated by My Illness*, Anatole Broyard quotes Ernest Becker as saying that we achieve immortality by being "insistently and inimitably ourselves." I don't know if immortality is achieved, but when we are our most essential selves, we are most fully alive, and that, at least, is at the opposite end of the spectrum from death.

Belinda is insistently herself. It may be comfortingly anthropomorphic to imagine her as the herd mother—we want our mothers to have our best interests at heart—but it is probably more accurate to see her as an individual committed to her own interests. To my sometime distress, Mother was insistently herself, too. It was difficult to be the daughter of someone who was insistently herself, but perhaps because of Mother's example, I am resolutely drawn to become my own inimitable self. What I call ruthlessness in Belinda and in myself instead may be a sort of whittling away of what is not-us, a paring down to our very pith—stripping away distractions, killing off occasions for trivial emotions. What's essential to me now is very simple—walking with the dogs and sitting with the goats, soaking up the colors of one more autumn, reading, and writing my self into existence.

Here's what I picture: Becoming as concentrated as a diamond. Lest that call to mind immoderate self-regard, the word *nubbin* is as graphic. After all the fluff's gone, I'll be a kernel, thoroughly myself through and through, reduced to my least divisible self, an adamantine core. All that can be divided has been divided and what is left is the number one—the irreducible *I*—the only thing with which to assert life against the bleak inevitability of death.

You wouldn't expect to receive one of life's great lessons during a regular dental prophylaxis, but a few months ago I found myself in the dentist's chair, my mouth open, tears leaking into it. My hygienist was describing the recent death of her beloved dog. It was the same week Teddy died, so my tears were ready. For weeks after putting down her old dog, my hygienist had grieved. Then one day, her husband, a police detective in a small city outside of Binghamton, New York, a man with uncommon perspicacity, brought home a puppy. His wife reached out eagerly to accept the wriggling springer spaniel. Her husband held the puppy back for a few seconds and looked into his wife's eyes.

"There is a beginning and there is an end," he said gently. Then, placing the plump ball of flesh and fur in her arms, he said, "This is the beginning."

Acknowledgements

Many thanks to

—the readers of *Laying Foundations*, whose enthusiastic
      responses to that book gave me the encouragement
      necessary to put together a second one

—my sister Penny, whose generous birthday and Christmas
      gifts over the years have amounted to a virtual
      writing endowment

—Madeline Gutin Perri, first guest at the Gray Ghost Guest
      House, spotter of the scarlet tanager, and
      punctilious copyeditor where punctiliousness
      is a plus

—my dear H, indefatigable fellow homemaker,
      the "go for it" guy

About the Author

Lucy Wilson Sherman's essays have appeared in *Creative Nonfiction* and *Pilgrimage*. "Learning from Goats" was included in *On Nature: Great Writers on the Great Outdoors*. She received a Master of Fine Arts in creative nonfiction from Goddard College.

Sherman is the author of a memoir, *Laying Foundations: A Year Building a Life While Rebuilding a Farmhouse*. She lives in Susquehanna, Pennsylvania, with her husband, and is at work on an autobiography titled *Inside Out*.